Charlotte Mary Yonge

A reputed Changeling

Or, Three seventh Years two Centuries ago - Vol. I

Charlotte Mary Yonge

A reputed Changeling
Or, Three seventh Years two Centuries ago - Vol. I

ISBN/EAN: 9783337111939

Printed in Europe, USA, Canada, Australia, Japan

Cover: Foto ©ninafisch / pixelio.de

More available books at **www.hansebooks.com**

A
REPUTED CHANGELING

OR

THREE SEVENTH YEARS TWO
CENTURIES AGO

BY

CHARLOTTE M. YONGE

IN TWO VOLUMES

VOL. I

London
MACMILLAN AND CO.
AND NEW YORK
1889

All rights reserved

PREFACE

I DO not think I have here forced the hand of history except by giving Portchester to two imaginary Rectors, and by a little injustice to her whom Princess Anne termed 'the brick-bat woman.'

The trial is not according to present rules, but precedents for its irregularities are to be found in the doings of the seventeenth century, notably in the trial of Spencer Cowper by the same Judge Hatsel, and I have done my best to represent the habits of those country gentry who were not infected by the evils of the later Stewart reigns.

There is some doubt as to the proper spelling of Portchester, but, judging by analogy, the *t* ought not to be omitted.

C. M. YONGE.

2d May 1889.

CONTENTS

CHAPTER I
THE EXPERIENCES OF GOODY MADGE
PAGE
1

CHAPTER II
HIGH TREASON . . 17

CHAPTER III
THE FAIRY RING . 39

CHAPTER IV
IMP OR NO IMP . 51

CHAPTER V
PEREGRINE'S HOME . 74

CHAPTER VI
A RELAPSE . . 88

CHAPTER VII
THE ENVOY . 103

CHAPTER VIII
THE RETURN . . 124

CHAPTER IX
ON HIS TRAVELS . . 148

CHAPTER X
THE MENAGERIE 162

CHAPTER XI
PROPOSALS . 186

CHAPTER XII
THE ONE HOPE . 217

CHAPTER XIII
THE BONFIRE . 245

CHAPTER XIV
GATHERING MOUSE-EAR . 256

CHAPTER XV
NEWS FROM FAREHAM . 266

CHAPTER XVI
A ROYAL NURSERY 279

CHAPTER XVII
MACHINATIONS . . . 295

CHAPTER XVIII
HALLOWMAS EVE . . 317

CHAPTER I

THE EXPERIENCES OF GOODY MADGE

> 'Dear Madam, think me not to blame;
> Invisible the fairy came.
> Your precious babe is hence conveyed,
> And in its place a changeling laid.
> Where are the father's mouth and nose,
> The mother's eyes as black as sloes?
> See here, a shocking awkward creature,
> That speaks a fool in every feature.'
> GAY.

'HE is an ugly, ill-favoured boy—just like *Riquet à la Houppe.*'

'That he is! Do you not know that he is a changeling?'

Such were the words of two little girls walking home from a school for young ladies kept, at the Cathedral city of Winchester, by two Frenchwomen of quality, refugees from the persecutions preluding the Revocation of the Edict of Nantes, and who enlivened the studies of their pupils with the *Contes de Commère L'Oie.*

The first speaker was Anne Jacobina Woodford, who had recently come with her mother, the widow of a brave naval officer, to live with her uncle, the Prebendary then in residence. The other was Lucy Archfield, daughter to a knight, whose home was a few miles from Portchester, Dr. Woodford's parish on the southern coast of Hampshire.

In the seventeenth century, when roads were mere ditches often impassable, and country-houses frequently became entirely isolated in the winter, it was usual with the wealthier county families to move into their local capital, where some owned mansions and others hired prebendal houses, or went into lodgings in the roomy dwellings of the superior tradesmen. For the elders this was the season of social intercourse, for the young people, of education.

The two girls, who were about eight years old, had struck up a rapid friendship, and were walking hand in hand to the Close attended by the nurse in charge of Mistress Lucy. This little lady wore a black silk hood and cape, trimmed with light brown fur, and lined with pink; while Anne Woodford, being still in mourning for her father, was wrapped in a black cloak, unrelieved except by the white border of her round cap, fringed by fair curls, contrasting with her brown eyes. She was taller and had a more upright bearing of head and neck, with more promise of beauty than her companion, who was much more countrified and would not have been taken for the child of higher station.

They had traversed the graveyard of the Cathedral, and were passing through a narrow archway known as the Slype, between the south-western angle of the Cathedral and a heavy mass of old masonry forming part of the garden wall of the present abode of the Archfield family, when suddenly both children stumbled and fell, while an elfish peal of laughter sounded behind them.

Lucy came down uppermost, and was scarcely hurt, but Anne had fallen prone, striking her chin on the ground, so as to make her bite her lip, and bruising knees and elbows severely. Nurse detected the cause of the fall so as to avoid it herself. It was a cord fastened across the archway, close to the ground, and another shout of derision greeted the discovery; while Lucy, regaining her feet, beheld for a moment a weird exulting grimace on a visage peeping over a neighbouring headstone.

'It is he! it is he! The wicked imp! There's no peace for him! I say,' she screamed, 'see if you don't get a sound flogging!' and she clenched her little fist as the provoking 'Ho! ho! ho!' rang farther and farther off. 'Don't cry, Anne dear; the Dean and Chapter shall take order with him, and he shall be soundly beaten. Are you hurt? O nurse, her mouth is all blood.'

'I hope she has not broken a tooth,' said nurse, who had been attending to the sobbing child. 'Come in, my lamb, we will wash your face and make you well.'

Anne, blinded with tears, jarred, bruised, bleeding, and bewildered, submitted to be led by kind nurse the more willingly because she knew that her mother, together with all the quality, were at Sir Thomas Charnock's. They had dined at the fashionable hour of two, and were to stay till supper-time, the elders playing at Ombre, the juniors dancing. As a rule the ordinary clergy did not associate with the county families, but Dr. Woodford was of good birth and a royal chaplain, and his deceased brother had been a favourite officer of the Duke of York, and had been so severely wounded by his side in the battle of Southwold as to be permanently disabled. Indeed Anne Jacobina was godchild to the Duke and his first Duchess, whose favoured attendant her mother had been. Thus Mrs. Woodford was in great request, and though she had not hitherto gone into company since her widowhood, she had yielded to Lady Charnock's entreaty that she would come and show her how to deal with that strange new Chinese infusion, a costly packet of which had been brought to her from town by Sir Thomas, as the Queen's favourite beverage, wherewith the ladies of the place were to be regaled and astonished.

It had been already arranged that the two little girls should spend the evening together, and as they entered the garden before the house a rude voice exclaimed, 'Holloa! London Nan whimpering. Has my fine lady met a spider or a cow?' and a big rough lad of twelve, in a college gown, spread out his arms, and danced up and down in the doorway to bar the entrance.

'Don't, Sedley,' said a sturdy but more gentlemanlike lad of the same age, thrusting him aside. 'Is she hurt? What is it?'

'That spiteful imp, Peregrine Oakshott,' said Lucy passionately. 'He had a cord across the Slype to trip us up. I heard him laughing like a hobgoblin, and saw him too, grinning over a tombstone like the malicious elf he is.'

The college boy uttered a horse laugh, which made Lucy cry, 'Cousin Sedley, you are as bad!' but the other boy was saying, 'Don't cry, Anne None-so-pretty. I'll give it him well! Though I'm younger, I'm bigger, and I'll show him reason for not meddling with my little sweetheart.'

'Have with you then!' shouted Sedley, ready for a fray on whatever pretext, and off they rushed, as nurse led little Anne up the broad shallow steps of the dark oak staircase, but Lucy stood laughing with exultation in the intended vengeance, as her brother took down her father's hunting-whip.

'He must be wellnigh a fiend to play such wicked pranks under the very Minster!' she said.

'And a rascal of a Whig, and that's worse,' added Charles; 'but I'll have it out of him!'

'Take care, Charley; if you offend him, and he does really belong to those—those creatures'—Lucy lowered her voice—'who knows what they might do to you?'

Charles laughed long and loud. 'I'll take care of that,' he said, swinging out at the door. 'Elf or no elf, he shall learn what it is to play off his tricks on *my* sister and my little sweetheart.'

Lucy betook herself to the nursery, where Anne was being comforted, her bleeding lip washed with essence, and repaired with a pinch of beaver from a hat, and her other bruises healed with lily leaves steeped in strong waters.

'Charley is gone to serve him out!' announced Lucy as the sovereign remedy.

'Oh, but perhaps he did not mean it,' Anne tried to say.

'Mean it? Small question of that, the cankered young slip! Nurse, do you think those he belongs to can do Charley any harm if he angers them?'

'I cannot say, missie. Only 'tis well we be not at home, or there might be elf knots in the horses' manes to-night. I doubt me whether *that sort* can do much hurt here, seeing as 'tis holy ground.'

'But is he really a changeling? I thought there were no such things as——'

'Hist, hist, Missie Anne!' cried the dame; ''tis not good to name them.'

'Oh, but we are on the Minster ground, nurse,' said Lucy, trembling a little however, looking over her shoulder, and coming closer to the old servant.

'Why do they think so?' asked Anne. 'Is it because he is so ugly and mischievous and rude? Not like boys in London.'

'Prithee, nurse, tell her the tale,' entreated Lucy, who had made large eyes over it many a time before.

'Ay, and who should tell you all about it save me, who had it all from Goody Madge Bulpett, as saw it all?'

'Goody Madge! It was she that came when poor little Kitty was born and died,' suggested Lucy, as Anne, laying her aching head upon nurse's knees, prepared to listen to the story.

'Well, deary darlings, you see poor Madam Oakshott never had her health since the Great Fire in London, when she was biding with her kinsfolk to be near Major Oakshott, who had got into trouble about some of his nonconforming doings. The poor lady had a mortal fright before she could be got out of Gracechurch Street as was all of a blaze, and she was so afeard of her husband being burnt as he lay in Newgate that she could scarce be got away, and whether it was that, or that she caught cold lying out in a tent on Highgate Hill, she has never had a day's health since.'

'And the gentleman—her husband?' asked Anne.

'They all broke prison, poor fellows, as they had need to do, and the Major's time was nearly up. He made himself busy in saving and helping the folk in the streets; and his brother, Sir Peregrine, who was thick with the King, and is in foreign parts now, took the chance to speak of the poor lady's plight and say it would be the death of her if he could not get his discharge, and his Majesty, bless his kind heart, gave the order at once. So they took madam home to the Chace, but she has been but an ailing body ever since.'

'But the fairy, the fairy, how did she change the babe?' cried Anne.

'Hush, hush, dearie! name them not. I am coming to it all in good time. I was telling you how the poor lady failed and pined from that hour, and was like to die. My gossip Madge told me how when, next Midsummer, this unlucky babe was born they had to take him from her chamber at once because any sound of crying made her start in her sleep, and shriek that she heard a poor child wailing who had been left in a burning house. Moll Owens, the hind's wife, a comely lass, was to nurse him, and they had him at once to her in the nursery, where was the elder child, two years old, Master Oliver, as you know well, Mistress Lucy, a fine-grown, sturdy little Turk as ever was.'

'Yes, I know him,' answered Lucy; 'and if his brother's a changeling, he is a bear! The Whig bear is what Charley calls him.'

'Well, what does that child do but trot out of the nursery, and try to scramble down the stairs.—Never tell me but that they you wot of trained him out—not that they had power over a Christian child, but that they might work their will on the little one. So they must needs trip him up, so that he rolled down the stair hollering and squalling all the way enough to bring the house down, and his poor lady mother, she woke up in a fit. The womenfolk ran, Molly and all, she being but a slip of a girl herself and giddy-pated, and when they came back after quieting Master Oliver, the babe was changed.'

'Then they didn't see the——'

'Hush, hush, missie! no one never sees 'em or they couldn't do nothing. They cannot, if a body is looking. But what had been as likely a child before as you would wish to handle was gone! The poor little mouth was all of a twist, and his eyelid drooped, and he never ceased mourn, mourn, mourn, wail, wail, wail, day and night, and whatever food he took he never was satisfied, but pined and peaked and dwined from day to day, so as his little legs was like knitting pins. The lady was nigh upon death as it seemed, so that no one took note of the child at first, but when Madge had time to look at him, she saw how it was, as plain as plain could be, and told his father. But men are unbelieving, my dears, and always think they know better than them as has the best right, and Major Oakshott would hear of no such thing, only if the boy was like to die, he must be christened. Well, Madge knew that sometimes they flee at touch of holy water, but no; though the thing mourned and moaned enough to curdle your blood and screeched out when the water touched him, there he was the same puny little canker. So when madam was better, and began to fret over the child that was nigh upon three months old, and no bigger than a newborn babe, Madge up and told her how it was, and the way to get her own again.'

'What was that, nurse?'

'There be different ways, my dear. Madge always held to breaking five and twenty eggs and have a pot boiling on a good sea-coal fire with the poker in it red hot, and then drop the shells in one by one, in sight of the creature in the cradle. Presently it will up and ask whatever you are about. Then you gets the poker in your hand as you says, " A-brewing of egg shells." Then it says, " I'm forty hunderd years old and odd, and yet I never heard of a-brewing of egg shells." Then you ups with the poker and at him to thrust it down his ugly throat, and there's a hissing and a whirling, and he is snatched away, and the real darling, all plump and rosy, is put back in the cradle.'

'And did they?'

'No, my dears. Madam was that soft-hearted she could not bring her mind to it, though they promised her not to touch him unless he spoke. But nigh on two years later, Master Robert was born, as fine and lusty and straight-limbed as a chrisom could be, while the other could not walk a step, but sat himself about on the floor, a-moaning and a-fretting with the legs of him for all the world like the drumsticks of a fowl, and his hands like claws, and his face wizened up like an old gaffer of a hunderd, or the jackanapes that Martin Boats'n brought from Barbary. So after a while madam saw the rights of it, and gave consent that means should be taken as Madge and other wise folk would have it; but he was too old by that time for the egg shells, for he could talk, talk, and ask questions enough to drive you wild. So they took him out under the privet hedge, Madge and her gossip Deborah Clint, and had got his clothes off to flog him with nettles till they changed him, when the ill-favoured elf began to squall and shriek like a whole litter of pigs, and as ill luck would have it, the master was within hearing, though they had watched him safe off to one of his own 'venticles, but it seems there had been warning that the justices were on the look-out, so home he came. And behold, the thing that never knew the use of his feet before, ups and flies at him, and lays hold of his leg, hollering out, "Sir, father, don't let them," and what not. So then it was all over with them, as though that were not proof enow what manner of thing it was! Madge tried to put him off with washing with yarbs being good for the limbs, but when he saw that Deb was there, he saith, saith he, as grim as may be, "Thou shalt not suffer a witch to live," which was hard, for she is but a white witch; and he stormed and raved at them with Bible texts, and then he vowed (men are so headstrong, my dears) that if ever he ketched them at it again, he would see Deb burnt for a witch at the stake, and Madge hung for the murder of the child, and he is well known to be a man of his word. So they had to leave him to abide by his bargain, and a sore handful he has of it.'

Anne drew a long sigh and asked whether the real boy in fairyland would never come back.

'There's no telling, missie dear. Some say they are bound there for ever and a day, some that they as holds 'em are bound to bring them back for a night once in seven years, and in the old times if they was sprinkled with holy water, and crossed, they would stay, but there's no such thing as holy water now, save among the Papists, and if one knew the way to cross oneself, it would be as much as one's life was worth.'

'If Peregrine was to die,' suggested Lucy.

'Bless your heart, dearie, he'll never die! When the true one's time comes, you'll see, if so be you be alive to see it, as Heaven grant, he will go off like the flame of a candle and nothing be left in his place but a bit of a withered sting nettle. But come, my sweetings, 'tis time I got your supper. I'll put some nice rosy-cheeked apples down to roast, to be soft for Mistress Woodford's sore mouth.'

Before the apples were roasted, Charles Archfield and his cousin, the colleger Sedley Archfield, a big boy in a black cloth gown, came in with news of having — together with the other boys, including Oliver and Robert Oakshott—hunted Peregrine all round the Close, but he ran like a lapwing, and when they had pinned him up in the corner by Dr. Ken's house, he slipped through their fingers up the ivy, and grinned at them over the wall like the imp he was. Noll said it was always the way, he was no more to be caught than a bit of thistledown, but Sedley meant to call out all the college boys and hunt and bait him down like a badger on 'Hills.'

CHAPTER II

HIGH TREASON

'Whate'er it be that is within his reach,
The filching trick he doth his fingers teach.'
Robin Badfellow.

THERE was often a considerable distance between children and their parents in the seventeenth century, but Anne Woodford, as the only child of her widowed mother, was as solace, comfort, and companion; and on her pillow in early morning the child poured forth in grave earnest the entire story of the changeling, asking whether he could not be 'taken to good Dr. Ken, or the Dean, or the Bishop to be ex—ex—— what is it, mother? Not whipped with nettles. Oh no! nor burnt with red-hot pokers, but have holy words said so that the right one may come back.'

'My dear child, did you really believe that old nurse's tale?'

'O madam, she *knew* it. The other old woman saw it! I always thought fairies and elves were only in tales, but Lucy's nurse knows it is true. And *he* is not a bit like other lads, mamma dear. He is lean and small, and his eyes are of different colours, look two ways at once, and his mouth goes awry when he speaks, and he laughs just like—like a fiend. Lucy and I call him *Riquet à la Houppe*, because he is just like the picture in Mademoiselle's book, with a great stubbly bunch of hair sticking out on one side, and though he walks a little lame, he can hop and skip like a grasshopper, faster than any of the boys, and leap up a wall in a moment, and grin—oh most frightfully. Have you ever seen him, mamma?'

'I think so. I saw a poor boy, who seemed to me to have had a stroke of some sort when he was an infant.'

'But, madam, that would not make him so spiteful and malicious!'

'If every one is against him and treats him as a wicked mischievous elf, it is only too likely to make him bitter and spiteful. Nay, Anne, if you come back stuffed with old wives' tales, I shall not allow you to go home with Lucy Archfield.'

The threat silenced Anne, who was a grave and rather silent little person, and when she mentioned it to her friend, the answer was, 'Did you tell your mother? If I had told mine, I should have been whipped for repeating lying tales.'

'Oh then you don't believe it!'

'It must be true, for Madge knew it. But that's the way always if one lets out that one knows more than they think.'

'It is not the way with my mother,' stoutly said Anne, drawing up her dignified little head. And she kept her resolution, for though a little excited by her first taste of lively youthful companionship, she was naturally a thoughtful reticent child, with a character advanced by companionship with her mother as an only child, through a great sorrow. Thus she was in every respect more developed than her contemporary Lucy, who regarded her with wonder as well as affection, and she was the object of the boyish devotion of Charley, who often defended her from his cousin Sedley's endeavours to put down what he considered upstart airs in a little nobody from London. Sedley teased and baited every weak thing in his way, and Lucy had been his chief butt till Anne Woodford's unconscious dignity and more cultivated manners excited his utmost spleen.

Lucy might be incredulous, but she was eager to tell that when her cousin Sedley Archfield was going back to 'chambers,' down from the Close gate came the imp on his shoulders in the twilight and twisted both legs round his neck, holding tight on in spite of plunges, pinches, and endeavours to scrape him off against the wall, which were frustrated or retaliated by hair pulling, choking, till just ere entering the college gateway, where Sedley looked to get his revenge among his fellows, he found his shoulders free, and heard 'Ho! ho! ho!' from the top of a wall close at hand. All the more was the young people's faith in the changeling story confirmed, and child-world was in those days even more impenetrable to their elders than at present.

Changeling or no, it was certain that

Peregrine Oakshott was the plague of the Close, where his father, an ex-officer of the Parliamentary army, had unwillingly hired a house for the winter, for the sake of medical treatment for his wife, a sufferer from a complication of ailments. Oakwood, his home, was about five miles from Dr. Woodford's living of Portchester, and as the families would thus be country neighbours, Mrs. Woodford thought it well to begin the acquaintance at Winchester. While knocking at the door of the house on the opposite side of the Close, she was aware of an elfish visage peering from an upper window. There was the queer mop of dark hair, the squinting light eyes, the contorted grin crooking the mouth, the odd sallow face, making her quite glad to get out of sight of the strange grimaces which grew every moment more hideous.

Mrs. Oakshott sat in an arm-chair beside a large fire in a wainscotted room, with a folding-screen shutting off the window. Her spinning-wheel was near, but it was only too plain that 'feeble was the hand, and silly the thread.' She bent her head in its wadded black velvet hood, but excused herself from rising, as she was crippled by rheumatic pains. She had evidently once been a pretty little person, innocent and inane, and her face had become like that of a withered baby, piteous in its expression of pain and weariness, but otherwise somewhat vacant. At first, indeed, there was a look of alarm. Perhaps she expected every visitor to come with a complaint of her unlucky Peregrine, but when Mrs. Woodford spoke cheerfully of being her neighbour in the country, she was evidently relieved and even gratified, prattling in a soft plaintive tone about her sufferings and the various remedies, ranging from woodlice rolled into natural pills, and grease off the church bells, to diamond dust and Goa stones, since, as she said, there was no cost to which Major Oakshott would not go for her benefit. He had even procured for her a pound of the Queen's new Chinese herb, and it certainly was as nauseous as could be wished, when boiled in milk, but she was told that was not the way it was taken at my Lady Charnock's. She was quite animated when Mrs. Woodford offered to show her how to prepare it.

Therewith the master of the house came in, and the aspect of affairs changed. He was a tall, dark, grave man, plainly though handsomely dressed, and in a gentlemanly way making it evident that visits to his wife were not welcome. He said that her health never permitted her to go abroad, and that his poor house contained nothing that could please a Court lady. Mrs. Oakshott shrank into herself, and became shy and silent, and Mrs. Woodford felt constrained to take leave, courteously conducted to the door by her unwilling host.

She had not taken many steps before she was startled by a sharp shower from a squirt coming sidelong like a blow on her cheek and surprising her into a low cry, which was heard by the Major, so that he hastened out, exclaiming, 'Madam, I trust that you are not hurt.'

'Oh no, sir! It is nothing—not a stone —only water!' she said, wiping it with her handkerchief.

'I am grieved and ashamed at the evil pranks of my unhappy son, but he shall suffer for it.'

'Nay, sir, I pray you. It was only childish mischief.'

He had not waited to hear her pleadings, and before she was half across the Close he had overtaken her, dragging the cowering struggling boy in his powerful grasp.

'Now, Peregrine,' he commanded, 'let me instantly hear you ask the lady's pardon for your dastardly trick. Or——!' and his other hand was raised for a blow.

'I am sure he is sorry,' said Mrs. Woodford, making a motion to ward off the stroke, and as the queer eyes glanced up at her in wondering inquiry, she laid her hand on the bony shoulder, saying, 'I know you did not mean to hurt me. You are sorry, are you not?'

'Ay,' the boy muttered, and she saw a look of surprise on his father's face.

'There,' she said, 'he has made his amends, and surely that may suffice.'

'Nay, madam, it would be a weak and ungodly tenderness that would spare to drive forth the evil spirit which possesses the child by the use of the rod. I should fail in my duty alike to God and man,' he added, in reply to a fresh gesture of intercession, 'did I not teach him what it is to insult a lady at mine own door.'

Mrs. Woodford could only go away, heartily sorry for the boy. From that time, however, both she and her little daughter were untouched by his tricks, though every one else had some complaint. Peas were shot from unknown recesses at venerable canons, mice darted out before shrieking ladies, frogs' clammy forms descended on the nape of their necks, hedgehogs were curled up on their chairs, and though Peregrine Oakshott was not often caught in the act, no mischief ever took place that was not attributed to him; and it was popularly believed in the Close that his father flogged him every morning for what he was about to do, and his tutor repeated the castigation every evening for what he had done, besides interludes at each detection.

Perhaps frequent usage had toughened his skin, or he had become expert in wriggling from the full force of the blow, or else, as many believed, the elfish nature was impervious; for he was as ready as ever for a trick the moment he was released, like, as his brother said, the dog Keeper, who, with a slaughtered chick hung round his neck in penance, rushed murderously upon the rest of the brood.

Yet Mrs. Woodford, on her way through the Cathedral nave, was aware of something leaning against one of the great columns, crouching together so that the dark head, supported on the arms, rested against the pillar which fluted the pier. The organ was pealing softly and plaintively, and the little gray coat seemed to heave as with a sob. She stood, impelled to offer to take him with her into the choir, but a verger, spying him, began rating him in a tone fit for expelling a dog, 'Come, master, none of your pranks here! Be not you ashamed of yourself to be lying in wait for godly folk on their way to prayers? If I catch you here again the Dean shall hear of it, and you shall smart for it.'

Mrs. Woodford began, 'He was only hearkening to the music,' but she caught such a look of malignity cast upon the verger as perfectly appalled her, and in another moment the boy had dashed, head over heels, out at the nearest door.

The next report that reached her related how a cloud of lime had suddenly descended from a broken arch of the cloister on the solemn verger, on his way to escort the Dean to the Minster, powdering his wig, whitening his black gown from collar to hem, and not a little endangering his eyesight.

The culprit eluded all pursuit on this occasion; but Mrs. Woodford soon after was told that the Major had caught Peregrine listening at the little south door of the choir, had collared him, and flogged him worse than ever, for being seduced by the sounds of the popish and idolatrous worship, and had told all his sons that the like chastisement awaited them if they presumed to cross the threshold of the steeple house.

Nevertheless the Senior Prefect of the college boys, when about to come out of the Cathedral on Sunday morning, found his gown pinned with a skewer so fast to the seat that he was only set free at the expense of a rent. Public opinion decided that the deed had been done by the imp of Oakshott, and accordingly the whole of the Wykeham scholars set on him with hue and cry the first time they saw him outside the Close, and hunted him as far as St. Cross, where he suddenly and utterly vanished from their sight.

Mrs. Woodford agreed with Anne that it was a very strange story. For how could he have been in the Cathedral at service time when it was well known that Major Oakshott had all his family together at his own form of worship in his house? Anne, who had been in hopes that her mother would be thus convinced of his supernatural powers, looked disappointed; but she had afterwards to confess that Charles Archfield had found out that it was his cousin Sedley Archfield who had played the audacious trick, in revenge for a well-merited tunding from the Prefect.

'And then saddled it on young Oakshott?' asked her mother.

'Charley says one such matter more or less makes no odds to the Whig ape; but I cannot endure Sedley Archfield, mamma.'

'If he lets another lad bear the blame of his malice he cannot indeed be a good lad.'

'So Charley and Lucy say,' returned Anne. 'We shall be glad to be away from Winchester, for while Peregrine Oakshott torments slyly, Sedley Archfield loves to frighten us openly, and to hurt us to see how much we can bear, and if Charley tries to stand up for us, Sedley calls him a puny wench and a milksop, and knocks him down. But, dear madam, pray do not tell what I have said to her ladyship, for there is no knowing what Sedley would do to us.'

'My little maid has not known before what boys can be!'

'No; but indeed Charles Archfield is quite different; almost as if he had been bred in London. He is a very gentleman. He never is rude to any girl, and he is courteous and gentle and kind. He gathered walnuts for us yesterday, and cracked all mine, and I am to make him a purse with two of the shells.'

Mrs. Woodford smiled, but there was a short thrill of anxiety in her motherly heart as her glance brought up a deeper colour into Anne's cheeks. There was a reserve to bring that glow, for the child knew that if she durst say that Charles called her his little sweetheart and wife, and that the walnut-shell purse would be kept as a token, she should be laughed at as a silly child, perhaps forbidden to make it, or else her uncle might hear and make a joke of it. It was not exactly disingenuousness, but rather the first dawn of maidenly reserve and modesty that reddened her cheek in a manner her mother did not fail to observe.

Yet it was with more amusement than misgiving, for children played at courtship like other games in mimicry of being grown up, and a baronet's only son was in point of fact almost as much out of the reach of a sea-captain's daughter and clergyman's niece as a prince of the blood royal; and Master Archfield would probably be contracted long before he could choose for himself, for his family were not likely to take into account that if Captain Woodford had not been too severely wounded to come forward after the battle of Southwold Bay he would have been knighted. On the strength of which Anne, as her companions sometimes said, gave herself in consequence more airs than Mistress Lucy ever did.

Sedley, a poor cousin, a destitute Cavalier's orphan, who had been placed on the foundation at Winchester College in hopes that he might be provided for in the Church, would have been far more on her level; and indeed Lady Archfield, a notable matchmaker, had already hinted how suitable such a thing would be. However, the present school character of Master Sedley, as well as her own observations, by no means inclined Mrs. Woodford towards the boy, large-limbed and comely-faced, but with a bullying, scowling air that did not augur well for his wife or his parish.

Whether it were this lad's threats, or, more likely, the fact that all the Close was on the alert, Peregrine's exploits were less frequent there, and began to extend to the outskirts of the city. There were some fine yew-trees on the southern borders, towards the chalk down, with massive dark foliage upon stout ruddy branches, among which Peregrine, armed with a fishing-rod, line, and hook, sat perched, angling for what might be caught from unconscious passengers along a path which led beneath.

From a market-woman's basket he abstracted thus a fowl! His 'Ho! ho! ho!' startled her into looking up, and seeing it apparently resuscitated, and hovering aloft. Full of dismay, she hurried shrieking away to tell the story of the bewitched chick at the market-cross among her gossips.

His next capture was a chop from a butcher boy's tray, but this involved more peril, for with a fierce oath that he would be revenged on the Whiggish imp, the lad darted at the tree; in vain, however, for Peregrine had dropped down on the other side, and crept unseen to another bush, where he lay *perdu*, under the thick green branches, rod and all, while the youth, swearing and growling, was shaking his former refuge.

As soon as the coast was clear he went back to his post, and presently was aware of three gentlemen advancing over the down, pointing, measuring, and surveying. One was small and slight, as simply dressed as a gentleman of the period could be; another was clad in a gay coat with a good deal of fluttering ribbon and rich lace; the third, a tall, well-made man, had a plain walking suit, surmounted by a flowing periwig and plumed beaver. Coming close beneath Peregrine's tree, and standing with their backs to it, they eagerly conversed. 'Such a cascade will drown the honours of the Versailles fountains, if only the water can be raised to such a height. Are you sure of it, Wren?'

'As certain as hydraulics can make me, sir;' and the lesser man began drawing lines with his stick in the dust of the path in demonstration.

The opportunity was irresistible, and the hook from above deftly caught the band of the feathered hat of the taller man, slowly and steadily drawing it up, entirely unperceived by the owner, on whose wig it had rested, and who was bending over the dust-traced diagram in absorbed attention. Peregrine deferred his hobgoblin laughter, for success emboldened him farther. Detaching the hat from his hook, and depositing it safely in a fork of the tree, he next cautiously let down his line, and contrived to get a strong hold of one of the black locks on the top of the wig, just as the wearer was observing, 'Oliver's Battery, eh? A cupola with a light to be seen out at sea? Our sailors will make another St. Christopher of you! Ha! what's this?'

For feeling as if a branch were touching the structure on his head, he had stepped forward, thus favouring Peregrine's manœuvres so that the wig dangled in the air, suddenly disclosing the bare skull of a very dark man, with such marked features that it needed not the gentleman's outcry to show the boy who was the victim of his mischief.

'What imp is there?' cried the King, spying up into the tree, while his attendant drew his sword, 'How now?' as Peregrine half climbed, half tumbled down, bringing hat and wig with him, and, whether by design or accident, fell at his feet. 'Will nothing content you but royal game?' he continued laughing, as Sir Christopher Wren helped him to resume his wig. 'Why, what a shrimp it is! a mere goblin sprite! What's thy name, master wag?'

'Peregrine Oakshott, so please you,' the boy answered, raising himself with a face scared indeed, but retaining its queer impishness. 'Sir, I never guessed——'

'Young rogue! have you our licence to waylay our loyal subjects?' demanded the King, with an affected fierceness. 'Know you not 'tis rank treason to discrown our sacred Majesty, far more to dishevel or destroy our locks? Why! I might behead you on the spot.'

To his great amazement the boy, with an eager face and clasped hands, exclaimed, 'O sir! Oh, please your Majesty, do so.'

'Do so!' exclaimed the King astounded. 'Didst hear what I said?'

'Yes, sir! You said it was a beheading matter, and I'm willing, sir.'

'Of all the petitions that ever were made to me, this is the strangest!' exclaimed Charles. 'An urchin like this weary of life! What next? So,' with a wink to his companions, 'Peregrine Oakshott, we condemn thee for high treason against our most sacred Majesty's beaver and periwig, and sentence thee to die by having thine head severed from thy body. Kneel down, open thy collar, bare thy neck. Ay, so, lay thy neck across that bough. Killigrew, do thy duty.'

To the general surprise, the boy complied

with all these directions, never flinching nor showing sign of fear, except that his lips were set and his cheek whitened. As he knelt, with closed eyes, the flat cold blade descended on his neck, the tension relaxed, and he sank!

'Hold!' cried the King. 'It is gone too far! He has surely not carried out the jest by dying on our hands.'

'No, no, sir,' said Wren, after a moment's alarm, 'he has only swooned. Has any one here a flask of wine to revive him?'

Several gentlemen had come up, and as Peregrine stirred, some wine was held to his lips, and he presently asked in a faint voice, 'Is this fairyland?'

'Not yet, my lad,' said Charles, 'whatever it may be when Wren's work is done.'

The boy opened his eyes, and as he beheld the same face, and the too familiar sky and trees, he sighed heavily, and said, 'Then it is all the same! O sir, would you but have cut off my head in good earnest, I might be at home again!'

'Home! what means the elf?'

'An elf! That is what they say I am—changed in the cradle,' said Peregrine, incited to confidence by the good-natured eyes, 'and I thought if I were close on death mine own people might take me home, and bring back the right one.'

'He really believes it!' exclaimed Charles much diverted. 'Tell me, good Master Elf, who is thy father, I mean not my brother Oberon, but him of the right one, as thou sayst.'

'Mr. Robert Oakshott of Oakwood, sir,' said Peregrine.

'A sturdy squire of the country party,' said the King. 'I am much minded to secure the lad for an elfin page,' he added aside to Killigrew. 'There's a fund of excellent humour and drollery in those queer eyes of his! So, Sir Hobgoblin, if you are proof against cold steel, I know not what is to be done with you. Get you back, and devise some other mode of finding your way home to fairyland.'

Peregrine said not a word of his adventure, so that the surprise of his family was the greater when overtures were made through Sir Christopher Wren for his appointment as a royal page.

'I would as soon send my son at once to be a page to Beelzebub,' returned Major Oakshott.

And though Sir Christopher did not return the answer exactly in those terms, he would not say that the Puritan Major did not judge rightly.

CHAPTER III

THE FAIRY RING

' She's turned her right and round about,
   And thrice she blew on a grass-green horn,
And she sware by the moon and the stars above
   That she'd gar me rue the day I was born.'
                    Old Ballad of Alison Cross.

DR. WOODFORD's parish was Portchester, where stood the fine old royal castle at present ungarrisoned, and partly dismantled in the recent troubles, on a chalk peninsula, a spur from Portsdown, projecting above the alluvial flats, and even into the harbour, whose waves at high tide laved the walls. The church and churchyard were within the ample circuit of the fortifications, about two furlongs distant from the main building, where rose the mighty Norman keep, above the inner court, with a gate tower at this date, only inhabited by an old soldier as porter with his family. A massive square tower at each angle of the huge wall likewise defied decay.

It was on Midsummer eve, that nearly about sundown, Dr. Woodford was summoned by the severe illness of the gatekeeper's old father, and his sister-in-law went with him to attempt what her skill could accomplish for the old man's relief.

They were detained there till the sun had long set, though the air, saturated with his redness, was full of soft twilight, while the moon, scarcely past the full, was just high enough to silver the quiet sea, and throw the shadow of the battlements and towers on the sward whitened with dew.

After the close atmosphere of the sickroom the freshness was welcome, and Mrs. Woodford, once a friend of Katherine Phillips, 'the Matchless Orinda,' had an eye and a soul to appreciate the beauty, and she even murmured the lines of *Il Penseroso* as she leant on the arm of her brother-in-law, who, in his turn, thought of Homer.

Suddenly, as they stood in the shadow, they were aware of a small, slight, fantastic figure in the midst of the grass-grown court, where there was a large green mushroom circle or fairy ring. On the borders of this ring it paused with an air of disappointment. Then entering it stood still, took off the hat, whose lopsided appearance had given so strange an outline, and bowed four times in opposite directions, when, as the face was turned towards the spectators, invisible in the dark shadow, the lady recognised Peregrine Oakshott. She pressed the Doctor's arm, and they both stood still watching the boy bathing his hand in the dew, and washing his face with it, then kneeling on one knee, and clasping his hands, as he cried aloud in a piteous chant—

'Fairy mother, fairy mother! Oh, come, come and take me home! My very life is sore to me. They all hate me! My brothers and the servants, every one of them. And my father and tutor say I am possessed with an evil spirit, and I am beaten daily, and more than daily. I can never, never get a good word from living soul! This is the second seven years, and Midsummer night! Oh, bring the other back again! I'm weary,

I'm weary! Good elves, good elves, take me home. Fairy mother! Come, come, come!' Shutting his eyes he seemed to be in a state of intense expectation. Tears filled Mrs. Woodford's eyes. The Doctor moved forward, but no sooner did the boy become conscious of human presence than he started up, and fled wildly towards a postern door, but no sooner had he disappeared in the shadow than there was a cry and a fall.

'Poor child!' exclaimed Dr. Woodford, 'he has fallen down the steps to the vault. It is a dangerous pitfall.'

They both hurried to the place, and found the boy lying on the steps leading down to the vault, but motionless, and when they succeeded in lifting him up, he was quite unconscious, having evidently struck his head against the mouth of the vault.

'We must carry him home between us,' said Mrs. Woodford. 'That will be better than rousing Miles Gateward, and making a coil.'

Dr. Woodford, however, took the entire weight, which he declared to be very slight. 'No one would think the poor child fourteen years old,' he observed, 'yet did he not speak of a second seven ?'

'True,' said Mrs. Woodford, 'he was born after the Great Fire of London, which, as I have good cause to know, was in the year '66.'

There was still little sign of revival about the boy when he had been carried into the Parsonage, undressed and laid in the Doctor's own bed, only a few moans when he was handled, and on his thin, sharp features there was a piteous look of sadness entirely unlike his ordinary expression of malignant fun, and which went to the kind hearts of the Doctor and Mrs. Woodford. After exhausting their own remedies, as soon as the early daylight was available Dr. Woodford called up a couple of servants, and sent one into Portsmouth for a surgeon, and another to Oakwood to the parents.

The doctor was the first to arrive, though not till the morning was well advanced. He found that three ribs were broken against the edge of the stone step, and the head severely injured, and having had sufficient experience in the navy to be a reasonably safe practitioner, he did nothing worse than bleed the patient, and declared that absolute rest was the only hope of recovery.

He was being regaled with cold roast pig and ale when Major Oakshott rode up to the door. Four horses were dragging the great lumbering coach over Portsdown hill, but he had gone on before, to thank Dr. and Mrs. Woodford for their care of his unfortunate son, and to make preparations for his transport home under the care of his wife's own woman, who was coming in the coach in the stead of the invalid lady.

'Nay, sir. Master Brent here has a word to say to that matter,' replied the Doctor.

'Truly, sir, I have,' said the surgeon; 'in his present state it is as much as your son's life is worth to move him.'

'Be that as it may seem to man, he is in the hand of Heaven, and he ought to be at home, whether for life or death.'

'For death it will assuredly be, sir, if he be jolted and shaken along the Portsdown roads—yea, I question whether you would get him to Oakwood alive,' said Brent, with naval roughness.

'Indeed, sir,' added Mrs. Woodford, 'Mrs. Oakshott may be assured of my giving him as tender care as though he were mine own son.'

'I am beholden to you, madam,' said the Major; 'I know your kindliness of heart; but in good sooth, the unhappy and rebellious lad merits chastisement rather than pity, since what should he be doing at this distance from home, where he was shut up for his misdemeanours, save fleeing like the Prodigal of the parable, or else planning another of his malicious pranks, as I greatly fear, on you or your daughter, madam. If so, he hath fallen into the pit that he made for others.'

The impulse was to tell what had occurred, but the surgeon's presence, and the dread of making all worse for the poor boy checked both the hosts, and Mrs. Woodford only declared that since the day of the apology he had never molested her or her little girl.

'Still,' said the Major, 'it is not possible to leave him in a stranger's house, where at any moment the evil spirit that is in him may break forth.'

'Come and see him, and judge,' said Dr. Woodford.

When the father beheld the deathly face and motionless form, stern as he was, he was greatly shocked. His heavy tread caused a moan, and when he said, 'What, Perry, how now?' there was a painful shrinking and twitching, which the surgeon greeted as evidence of returning animation, but which made him almost drag the Major out of the room for fear of immediate consequences.

Major Oakshott, and still more the servant, who had arrived in the coach and come upstairs, could not but be convinced that removal was not to be thought of. The maid was, moreover, too necessary to her mistress to be left to undertake the nursing, much to her master's regret, but to the joy of Mrs. Woodford, who felt certain that by far the best chance for the poor boy was in his entire separation from all associations with the home where he had evidently suffered so much.

There was, perhaps, nothing except the pageship at Court that could have gone more against Major Oakshott's principles than to leave his son in the house of a prelatical minister, but alternative there was none, and he could only express how much he was beholden to the Dr. and Mrs. Woodford.

All their desire was that he would remain at a distance, for during the long and weary watch they had to keep over the half-conscious lad, the sound of a voice or even a horse's tread from Oakwood occasioned moans and restlessness. The Major rode over, or sent his sons or a servant daily to inquire during the first fortnight, except on the Sundays, and on each of these the patient made a step towards improvement.

At first he lay in a dull, deathlike stupor, only groaning if disturbed, but by and by there was a babbling murmur of words, and soon the sound of his brother's loud voice at the door, demanding from the saddle how it went to-day with Peregrine, caused a shriek of terror and such a fit of trembling that Mrs. Woodford had to go out and make a personal request that Oliver would never again speak under the window. To her great relief, when the balance between life and death had decidedly turned, the inquiries became less frequent, and could often be forestalled by sending messengers to Oakwood.

The boy usually lay still all day in the darkened room, only showing pain at light or noise, but at night he often talked and rambled a good deal. Sometimes it was Greek or Latin, sometimes whole chapters of Scripture, either denunciating portions or genealogies from the First Book of Chronicles, the polysyllabic names pouring from his mouth whenever he was particularly oppressed or suffering, so that when Mrs. Woodford had with some difficulty made out what they were, she concluded that they had been set as tasks of penance.

At other times Peregrine talked as if he absolutely believed himself in fairyland, accepting a strawberry or cherry as elfin food, promising a tester in Anne's shoe when she helped to change his pillow, or conversing in the style of Puck, or Robin Goodfellow, on intended pranks. Often he fancied himself the lubber fiend resting at the fire his hairy strength, and watching for cock-crow as the signal for flinging out-of-doors. It was wonderful how in the grim and strict Puritanical household he could have imbibed so much fairy lore, but he must have eagerly assimilated and recollected whatever he heard, holding them as tidings from his true kith and kin; and, indeed, when he was running on thus, Mrs. Woodford sometimes felt a certain awe and chill, as of the preternatural, and could hardly believe that he belonged to ordinary human nature. Either she or the Doctor always took the night-watch after the talking mood set in, for they could not judge of the effect it might have on any of the servants. Indeed they sometimes doubted whether this were not the beginning of permanent insanity, as the delusion seemed to strengthen with symptoms of recovery.

'Then,' said Dr. Woodford, 'Heaven help the poor lad!'

For sad indeed was the lot in those days of even the most harmless lunatic.

'Yet,' said the lady, 'I scarcely think anything can be worse than what he undergoes at home. When I hear the terror and misery of his voice, I doubt whether we did him any true kindness by hindering his father from killing him outright by the shaking of his old coach.'

'Nay, sister, we strove to do our duty, though it may be we have taken on ourselves a further charge.'

CHAPTER IV

IMP OR NO IMP

'But wist I of a woman bold
   Who thrice my brow durst sign,
I might regain my mortal mould,
   As fair a form as thine.'
                                   SCOTT.

AT last came a wakening with intelligence in the eyes. In the summer morning light that streamed through the chinks of the shutters Mrs. Woodford perceived the glance of inquiry, and when she brought some cool drink, a rational though feeble voice asked those first questions, 'Who? and where?'

'I am Mrs. Woodford, my dear child. You remember me at Winchester. You are at Portchester. You fell down and hurt yourself, but you are getting better.'

She was grieved to see the look of utter

disappointment and weariness that overspread the features, and the boy hardly spoke again all day. There was much drowsiness, but also depression, and more than once Mrs. Woodford detected tears, but at other times he received her attentions with smiles and looks of wondering gratitude, as though ordinary kindness and solicitude were so new to him that he did not know what to make of them, and perhaps was afraid of breaking a happy dream by saying too much.

The surgeon saw him, and declared him so much better that he might soon be taken home, recommending his sitting up for a little while as a first stage. Peregrine, however, seemed far from being cheered, and showed himself so unwilling to undergo the fatigue of being dressed, even when good Dr. Woodford had brought up his own large chair— the only approach to an easy one in the house—that the proposal was dropped, and he was left in peace for the rest of the day.

In the evening Mrs. Woodford was sitting by the window, letting her needlework drop as the light faded, and just beginning to doze, when her repose was broken by a voice saying, 'Madam.'

'Yes, Peregrine.'

'Come near, I pray. Will you tell no one?'

'No; what is it?'

In so low a tone that she had to bend over him: 'Do you know how the Papists cross themselves?'

'Yes, I have seen the Queen's confessor and some of the ladies make the sign.'

'Dear lady, you have been very good to me! If you would only cross me thrice, and not be afraid! They could not hurt you!'

'Who? What do you mean?' she asked, for fairy lore had not become a popular study, but comprehension came when he said in an awe-stricken voice, 'You know what I am.'

'I know there have been old wives' tales about you, my poor boy, but surely you do not believe them yourself.'

'Ah! if you will not believe them, there is no hope. I might have known. You were so good to me;' and he hid his face.

She took his unwilling hand and said, 'Be you what you will, my poor child, I am sorry for you, for I see you are very unhappy. Come, tell me all.'

'Nay, then you would be like the rest,' said Peregrine, 'and I could not bear that,' and he wrung her hand.

'Perhaps not,' she said gently, 'for I know that a story is afloat that you were changed in your cradle, and that there are folk ignorant enough to believe it.'

'They all *know* it,' he said impressively. 'My mother and brothers and all the servants. Every soul knows it except my father and Mr. Horncastle, and they will never hear a word, but will have it that I am possessed with a spirit of evil that is to be flogged out of me. Goody Madge and Moll Owens, they knew how it was at the first, and would fain have forced them—mine own people—to take me home, and bring the other back, but my father found it out and hindered them.'

'To save your life.'

'Much good does my life do me! Every one hates or fears me. No one has a word for me. Every mischance is laid on me. When the kitchen wench broke a crock, it was because I looked at it. If the keeper misses a deer, he swears at Master Perry! Oliver and Robert will not let me touch a thing of theirs; they bait me for a mooncalf, and grin when I am beaten for their doings. Even my mother quakes and trembles when I come near, and thinks I give her the creeps. As to my father and tutor, it is ever the rod with them, though I can learn my tasks far better than those jolter-heads Noll and Robin. I never heard so many kind words in all my life as you have given me since I have been lying here!'

He stopped in a sort of awe, for tears fell from her eyes, and she kissed his forehead.

'Will you not help me, good madam?' he entreated. 'I went down to Goody Madge, and she said there was a chance for me every seven years. The first went by, but this is my fourteenth year. I had a hope when the King spoke of beheading me, but he was only in jest, as I might have known. Then methought I would try what Midsummer night in the fairy ring would do, but that was in vain; and now you, who could cross me if you would, will not believe. Oh, will you not make the trial?'

'Alas! Peregrine, supposing I could do it in good faith, would you become a mere tricksy sprite, a thing of the elements, and yield up your hopes as a Christian soul, a child of God and heir of Heaven?'

'My father says I am an heir of hell.'

'No, no, never,' she cried, shuddering at his quiet way of saying it. 'You are flesh and blood, christened, and with the hope set before you.'

'The christening came too late,' he said. 'O lady, you who are so good and pitiful, let my mother get back her true Peregrine—a straight-limbed, comely dullard, such as would be welcome to her. She would bless and thank you, and for me, to be a Will-of-the-wisp, or what not, would be far better than the life I lead. Never did I know what my mother calls peace till I lay here.'

'Ah, Peregrine, poor lad, your value for peace and for my poor kindness proves that you have a human heart and are no elf.'

'Indeed, I meant to flit about and give

you good dreams, and keep off all that could hurt or frighten you,' he said earnestly.

'Only the human soul could feel so, dear boy,' she answered tenderly.

'And you *really* disbelieve—the other,' he said wistfully.

'This is what I verily believe, my child: that there were causes to make you weakly, and that you may have had some palsy stroke or convulsive fit perhaps at the moment you were left alone. Such would explain much of your oddness of face, which made the ignorant nurses deem you changed; and thus it was only your father who, by God's mercy, saved you from a miserable death, to become, as I trust, a good and true man, and servant of God.' Then answering a hopeless groan, she added, 'Yes, it is harder for you than for many. I see that these silly servants have so nurtured you in this belief that you have never even thought it worth while to strive for goodness, but supposed tricksomeness and waywardness a part of your nature.'

'The only pleasure in life is paying folk off,' said Peregrine, with a glitter in his eye. 'It serves them right.'

'And thus,' she said sadly, 'you have gone on hating and spiting, deeming yourself a goblin without hope or aim; but now you feel that you have a Christian soul you will strive with evil, you will so love as to win love, you will pray and conquer.'

'My father and Mr. Horncastle pray,' said Peregrine bitterly. 'I hate it! They go on for ever, past all bearing; I *must* do something—stand on my head, pluck some one's stool away, or tickle Robin with a straw, if I am birched the next moment. That's the goblin.'

'Yet you love the Minster music.'

'Ay! Father calls it rank Popery. I listened many a time he never guessed, hid away in the Holy Hole, or within old Bishop Wykeham's little house.'

'Ah, Peregrine, could an imp of evil brook to lie hidden in the Holy Hole behind the very altar?' said Mrs. Woodford. 'But I hear Nick bringing in supper, and I must leave you for the present. God in His mercy bless you, His poor child, and lead you in His ways.'

As she went Peregrine muttered, 'Is that a prayer? It is not like father's.'

She was anxious to consult her brother-in-law on the strange mood of her patient. She found that he had heard more than he had told her of what Major Oakshott deemed the hopeless wickedness of his son, the antics at prayers, the hatred of everything good, the spiteful tricks that were the family torment. No doubt much was due to the boy's entire belief in his own elfship, and these two good people seriously considered how to save him from himself.

'If we could only keep him here,' said Mrs. Woodford, 'I think we might bring him to have some faith and love in God and man.'

'You could, dear sister,' said the Doctor, smiling affectionately; 'but Major Oakshott would never leave his son in our house. He abhors our principles too much, and besides, it is too near home. All the servants have heard rumours of this cruel fable, and would ascribe the least misadventure to his goblin origin. I must ride over to Oakwood and endeavour to induce his father to remove him to safe and judicious keeping.'

Some days, however, elapsed before Dr. Woodford could do this, and in the meantime the good lady did her best to infuse into her poor young guest the sense that he had a human soul, responsible for his actions, and with hope set before him, and that he was not a mere frolicsome and malicious sprite, the creature of unreasoning impulse.

It was a matter only to be attempted by gentle hints, for though reared in a strictly religious household, Peregrine's ears seemed to have been absolutely closed, partly by nursery ideas of his own exclusion from the pale of humanity, partly by the harsh treatment that he was continually bringing on himself. Preachings and prayers to him only meant a time of intolerable restraint, usually ending in disgrace and punishment; Scripture and the Westminster Catechism contained a collection of tasks more tedious and irksome than the Latin and Greek Grammar; Sunday was his worst day of the week, and these repugnances, as he had been taught to believe, were so many proofs that he was a being beyond the power of grace.

Mrs. Woodford scrupled to leave him to

any one else on this first Sunday of his recovered consciousness, and in hopes of keeping him quiet through fatigue, she contrived that it should be the first day of his being dressed, and seated in the arm-chair, resting against cushions beside the open window, whence he could watch the church-goers, Anne in her little white cap, with her book in one hand, and a posy in the other, tripping demurely beside her uncle, stately in gown, cassock, and scarlet hood.

Peregrine could not refrain from boasting to his hostess how he had once grimaced from outside the church window at Havant, and at the women shrieking that the fiend was there. She would not smile, and shook her head sadly, so that he said, 'I would never do so here.'

'Nor anywhere, I hope.'

Whereupon, thinking better to please the churchwoman, he related how, when imprisoned for popping a toad into the soup, he had escaped over the leads, and had beaten a drum outside the barn, during a discourse of the godly tinker, John Bunyan, tramping and rattling so that all thought the troopers were come, and rushed out, tumbling one over the other, while he yelled out his 'Ho! ho! ho!' from the haystack where he had hidden.

'When you feel how kind and loving God is,' said Mrs. Woodford gravely, 'you will not like to disturb those who are doing Him honour.'

'Is He kind?' asked Peregrine. 'I thought He was all wrath and anger.'

She replied, 'The Lord is loving unto every man, and His mercy is over all His works.'

He made no answer. If he were sullen, this subsided into sleepiness, and when he awoke he found the lady on her knees going through the service with her Prayer-book. She encountered his wistful eyes, but no remark was made, though on her return from fetching him some broth, she found him peeping into her book, which he laid down hastily, as though afraid of detection.

She had to go down to the Sunday dinner, where, according to good old custom, half a dozen of the poor and aged were regaled with the parish priest and his household.

There she heard inquiries and remarks showing how widely spread and deeply rooted was the notion of Peregrine's elfish extraction. If Daddy Hoskins did ask after the poor young gentleman as if he were a human being, the three old dames present shook their heads, and while the more bashful only groaned, Granny Perkins demanded, 'Well, now, my lady, do he eat and sleep like other folk?'

'Exactly, granny, now that he's mending in health.'

'And don't he turn and writhe when there's prayers?'

Mrs. Woodford deposed to having observed no such demonstrations.

'Think of that now! Lauk-a-daisy! I've heard tell by my nevvy Davy, as is turnspit at Oak'ood, as how when there's prayers and expounding by Master Horncastle, as is a godly man, saving his Reverence's presence, he have seen him, have Davy—Master Perry, as they calls him, a-twisted round with his heels on the chair, and his head where his heels should be, and a grin on his face enough to give one a turn.'

'Did Davy never see a mischievous boy fidgeting at prayers?' asked the Doctor, who was nearer than she thought. 'If so, he has been luckier than I have been.'

There was a laugh, out of deference to the clergyman, but the old woman held to her point. 'Begging your Reverence's pardon, sir, there be more in this than we knows. They says up at Oakwood, there's no peace in the place for the spite of him, and when they thinks he is safe locked into his chamber, there he be a-clogging of the spit, or changing sugar into pepper, or making the stool break down under one. Oh, he be a strange one, sir, or summat worse. I have heerd him myself hollaing "Ho! ho! ho!" on the downs enough to make one's flesh creep.'

'I will tell you what he is, dame,' said the Doctor gravely. 'He is a poor child who had a fit in his cradle, and whom all around have joined in driving to folly, evil, and despair through your foolish superstitions. He is my guest, and I will have no more said against him at my table.'

The village gossips might be silenced by awe of the parson, but their opinion was unshaken; and Silas Hewlett, a weather-beaten sailor with a wooden leg, was bold enough to answer, 'Ay, ay, sir, you parsons and gentlefolk don't believe naught; but you've not seen what I have with my own two bodily eyes——' and this of course was the prelude to the history of an encounter with a mermaid, which alternated with the Flying Dutchman and a combat with the Moors, as regular entertainment at the Sunday meal.

When Mrs. Woodford went upstairs she was met by the servant Nicolas, declaring that she might get whom she would to wait on that there moon-calf, he would not go neist the spiteful thing, and exhibiting a swollen finger, stung by a dead wasp, which Peregrine had cunningly disposed on the edge of his empty plate.

She soothed the man's wrath, and healed his wound as best she might, ere returning to her patient, who looked at her with an impish grin on his lips, and yet human deprecation in his eyes. Feeling unprepared for discussion, she merely asked whether the dinner had been relished, and sat down to her book; but there was a grave, sorrowful expression on her countenance, and, after an interval of lying back uneasily in his chair, he exclaimed, 'It is of no use; I could not help it. It is my nature.'

'It is the nature of many lads to be mischievous,' she answered; 'but grace can cure them.'

Therewith she began to read aloud. She had bought the *Pilgrim's Progress* (the first part) from a hawker, and she was glad to have at hand something that could hardly be condemned as frivolous or prelatical. The spell of the marvellous book fell on Peregrine; he listened intently, and craved ever to hear more, not being yet able to read without pain and dizziness. He was struck by hearing that the dream of Christian's adventures had visited that same tinker, whose congregation his own wicked practices had broken up.

'He would take me for one of the hobgoblins that beset Master Christian.'

'Nay,' said Mrs. Woodford, 'he would say you were Christian floundering in the Slough of Despond, and deeming yourself one of its efts or tadpoles.'

He made no answer, but on the whole behaved so well that the next day Mrs. Woodford ventured to bring her little daughter in after having extracted a promise that there should be no tricks nor teasing, a pledge honourably kept.

Anne did not like the prospect of the interview. 'Oh, ma'am, don't leave me alone with him!' she said. 'Do you know what he did to Mistress Martha Browning, his own cousin, you know, who lives at Emsworth with her aunt? He put a horsehair slily round her glass of wine, and tipped it over her best gray taffeta, and her aunt whipped her for the stain. She never would say it was his doing, and yet he goes on teasing her the same as ever, though his brother Oliver found it out, and thrashed him for it; you know Oliver is to marry Mistress Martha.'

'My dear child, where did you hear all this?' asked Mrs. Woodford, rather overwhelmed with this flood of gossip from her usually quiet daughter.

'Lucy told me, mamma. She heard it from Sedley, who says he does not wonder at any one serving out Martha Browning, for she is as ugly as sin.'

'Hush, hush, Anne! Such sayings do not become a young maid. This poor lad has scarce known kindness. Every one's hand has been against him, and so his hand has been against every one. I want my little daughter to be brave enough not to pain and anger him by shrinking from him as if he were not like other people. We must teach him to be happy before we can teach him to be good.'

'Madam, I will try,' said the child, with a great gulp; 'only if you would be pleased not to leave me alone with him the first time!'

This Mrs. Woodford promised. At first the boy lay and looked at Anne as if she were a rare curiosity brought for his examination, and it took all her resolution, even to a heroic exertion of childish fortitude, not to flinch under the gaze of those queer eyes. However, Mrs. Woodford diverted the glances by producing a box of spillekins, and in the interest of the game the children became better acquainted.

Over their next day's game Mrs. Woodford left them, and Anne became at ease since Peregrine never attempted any tricks. She taught him to play at draughts, the elders thinking it expedient not to doubt whether such vanities were permissible at Oakwood.

Soon there was such merriment between them that the kind Doctor said it did his heart good to hear the boy's hearty natural laugh in lieu of the 'Ho! ho! ho!' of malice or derision.

They were odd conversations that used to take place between that boy and girl. The King's offer of a pageship had oozed out in the Oakshott family, and Peregrine greatly resented the refusal, which he naturally attributed to his father's Whiggery and spite at all things agreeable, and he was fond of discussing his wrongs and longings with Anne, who, from her childish point of view, thought the walls of Portchester and the sluggish creek a very bad exchange for her enjoyments at Greenwich, where she had lived during her father's years of broken health, after he had been disabled at Southwold by a wound which had prevented his being knighted by the Duke of York for his daring in the excitement of the critical moment, a fact which Mistress Anne never forgot, though she only knew it by hearsay, as it happened a few weeks after she was born, and her father always averred that he was thankful to have missed the barren and expensive honour, and that the *worst* which had come of his exploit was the royal sponsorship to his little maid.

Anne had, however, been the pet of her father's old friends, the sea captains, had played with the little Evelyns under the yew hedges of Says Court, had been taken to London to behold the Lord Mayor's show and more than one Court pageant, had been sometimes at the palaces as the plaything of the Ladies Mary and Anne of York, had been more than once kissed by their father, the Duke, and called a pretty little poppet, and had even shared with them a notable game at romps with their good-natured uncle the King, when she had actually caught him at Blind-man's-buff!

Ignorant as she was of evil, her old surroundings appeared to her delightful, and

Peregrine, bred in a Puritan home, was at fourteen not much more advanced than she was in the meaning of the vices and corruptions that he heard inveighed against in general or scriptural terms at home, and was only too ready to believe that all that his father proscribed must be enchanting. Thus they built castles together about brilliant lives at a Court of which they knew as little as of that at Timbuctoo.

There was another Court, however, of which Peregrine seemed to know all the details, namely, that of King Oberon and Queen Mab. How much was village lore picked up from Moll Owens and her kind, or how much was the work of his own imagination, no one could tell, probably not himself, certainly not Anne. When he appeared on intimate terms with Hip, Nip, and Skip, and described catching Daddy Long Legs to make a fence with his legs, or dwelt upon a terrible fight between two armies of elves mounted on grasshoppers and crickets, and armed with lances tipped with stings of bees and wasps, she would exclaim, 'Is it true, Perry?' and he would wink his green eye and look at her with his yellow one till she hardly knew where she was.

He would tell of his putting a hornet in a sluttish maid's shoe, which was credible, if scarcely meriting that elfish laughter which made his auditor shrink, but when he told of dancing over the mud banks with a lantern, like a Will-of-the-wisp, till he lured boats to get stranded, or horsemen to get stuck, in the hopeless mud, Anne never questioned the possibility, but listened with wide open eyes, and a restrained shudder, feeling as if under a spell. That mysterious childish feeling which dreads even what common sense forbids the calmer mind to believe, made her credit Peregrine, for the time at least, with strange affinities to the underground folk, and kept her under a strange fascination, half attraction, half repulsion, which made her feel as if she must obey and follow him if he turned those eyes on her, whether she were willing or not.

Nor did she ever tell her mother of these conversations. She had been rebuked once for repeating nurse's story of the changeling, and again for her shrinking from him; and this was quite enough in an essentially reserved, as well as proud and sensitive, nature, to prevent further confidences on a subject which she knew would be treated as a foolish fancy, bringing both herself and her companion into trouble.

CHAPTER V

PEREGRINE'S HOME

'For, at a word, be it understood,
He was always for ill and never for good.'
SCOTT.

A WEEK had passed since any of the family from Oakwood had come to make inquiries after the convalescent at Portchester, when Dr. Woodford mounted his sleek, sober-paced pad, and accompanied by a groom, rode over to make his report and tender his counsel to Major Oakshott. He arrived just as the great bell was clanging to summon the family to the mid-day meal, since he had reckoned on the Squire being more amenable as a 'full man,' especially towards a guest, and he was well aware that the Major was thoroughly a gentleman in behaviour even to those with whom he differed in politics and religion.

Accordingly there was a ready welcome at the door of the old red house, which was somewhat gloomy looking, being on the north side of the hill, and a good deal stifled with trees. In a brief interval the Doctor found himself seated beside the pale languid lady at the head of the long table, placed in a large hall, wainscotted with the blackest of oak, which seemed to absorb into itself all the light from the windows, large enough indeed but heavily mullioned, and with almost as much of leading as of octagons and lozenges —greenish glass—in them, while the coats of arms, repeated in upper portions and at the intersections of beams and rafters, were not more cheerful, being sable chevrons on an argent field. The crest, a horse shoe, was indeed azure, but the blue of this and of the coats of the serving-men only deepened the thunderous effect of the black. Strangely, however, among these sad-coloured men there moved a figure entirely different. A negro, white turbaned, and with his blue livery of a lighter shade, of fantastic make and relieved by a great deal of white and shining silver, so as to have an entirely different effect.

He placed himself behind the chair of Dr. Woodford's opposite neighbour, a shrewd business-like looking gentleman, soberly but handsomely dressed, with a certain foreign cut about his clothes, and a cravat of rich Flemish lace. He was presented to the Doctor as Major Oakshott's brother, Sir Peregrine. The rest of the party consisted of Oliver and Robert, sturdy, ruddy lads of fifteen and twelve, and their tutor, Mr. Horncastle, an elderly man, who twenty years before had resigned his living because he could not bring himself to accept all the Liturgy.

While Sir Peregrine courteously relieved his sister-in-law of the trouble of carving the gammon of bacon which accompanied the veal which her husband was helping, Dr. Woodford informed her of her son's progress towards recovery.

'Ah,' she said, 'I knew you had come to tell us that he is ready to be brought home;' and her tone was fretful.

'We are greatly beholden to you, sir,' said the Major from the bottom of the table. 'The boy shall be fetched home immediately.'

'Not so, sir, as yet, I beg of you. Neither his head nor his side can brook the journey for at least another week, and indeed my good sister Woodford will hardly know how to part with her patient.'

'She will not long be of that mind after Master Perry gets to his feet again,' muttered the chaplain.

'Indeed no,' chimed in the mother. 'There will be no more peace in the house when he is come back.'

'I assure you, madam,' said Dr. Woodford, 'that he has been a very good child, grateful and obedient, nor have I heard any complaints.'

'Your kindness, or else that of Mrs. Woodford, carries you far, sir,' answered his host.

'What? Is my nephew and namesake so peevish a scapegrace?' demanded the visitor.

On which anecdotes broke forth from all quarters. Peregrine had greased the already slippery oak stairs, had exchanged Oliver's careful exercise for a ribald broadsheet, had filled Mr. Horncastle's pipe with gunpowder, and mixed snuff with the chocolate specially prepared for the peculiar godly guest Dame Priscilla Waller. Every one had something to adduce, even the serving-men behind the chairs; and if Oliver and Robert did not add their quota, it was because absolute silence at meals was the rule for nonage. However, the subject was evidently distasteful to the father, who changed the conversation by asking his brother questions about the young Prince of Orange and the Grand Pensionary De Witt. For the gentleman had been acting as English attaché to the Embassy at the Hague, whence he had come on affairs of State to London, and after being knighted by Charles, had newly arrived at the old home, which he had scarcely seen since his brother's marriage. Dr. Woodford enjoyed his conversation, and his information on foreign politics, and the Major, though now and then protesting, was evidently proud of his brother.

When grace had been pronounced by the chaplain the lady withdrew to her parlour, the two boys, each with an obeisance and request for permission, departed for an hour's recreation, and Dr. Woodford intimated that he wished for some conversation with his host respecting the boy Peregrine.

'Let us discuss it here,' said Major Oakshott, turning towards a small table set in the deep bay window, and garnished with wine, fruit, and long slender glasses. 'Good Mr. Horncastle,' he added, as he motioned his guest to one of the four seats, 'is with me in all that concerns my children, and I desire my brother's counsel respecting the untoward lad with whom it has pleased Heaven to afflict me.'

When the glasses had been filled with claret Dr. Woodford uttered a diplomatic compliment on the healthful and robust appearance of the eldest and youngest sons, and asked whether any cause had been assigned for the difference between them and the intermediate brother.

'None, sir,' returned the father with a sigh, 'save the will of the Almighty to visit us for our sins with a son who has thus far shown himself one of the marred vessels doomed to be broken by the potter. It may be in order to humble me and prove me that this hath been laid upon me.'

The chaplain groaned acquiescence, but there was vexation in the brother's face.

'Sir,' said the Doctor, 'it is my opinion and that of my sister-in-law, an excellent, discreet, and devout woman, that the poor child would give you more cause for hope if the belief had not become fixed in his mind that he is really and truly a fairy elf—yes, in very sooth—a changeling!'

All the auditors broke out into exclamations that it was impossible that a boy of fourteen could entertain so absurb an idea, and the tutor evidently thought it a fresh proof of depravity that he should thus have tried to deceive his kind hosts.

In proof that Peregrine veritably believed it himself, Dr. Woodford related what he had witnessed on Midsummer night, mentioning how in delirium the boy had evidently believed himself in fairyland, and how disappointed he had been, on regaining his senses, to find himself on common earth; telling also of the adventure with the King, which Sir Christopher Wren had described to him, but of which Major Oakshott was unaware, though it explained the offer of the pageship.

He was a good deal struck by these revelations, proving misery that he had never suspected, though, as he said, he had often pleaded, ' Why will ye revolt more and more? ye *will* be stricken more and more.'

' Have you ever sought his confidence?' asked the travelled brother, a question evidently scarcely understood, for the reply was, ' I have always required of my sons to speak the truth, nor have they failed of late years save this unfortunate Peregrine.'

' And,' said Sir Peregrine, ' if the unlucky lad actually supposes himself to be no human being, admonitions and chastisements would naturally be vain.'

' I cannot believe it,' exclaimed the Major. ' 'Tis true, as I now remember, I once came on a couple of beldames, my wife's nurse and another, who has since been ducked for witchcraft, and found them about to flog the babe with nettles, and lay him in the thorn hedge because he was a sickly child, whom, forsooth, they took to be a changeling; but I forbade the profane folly to be ever again mentioned in my household, nor did I ever hear thereof again.'

'There are a good many more things mentioned in a household, brother, than the master is wont to hear of,' remarked Sir Peregrine.

Dr. Woodford then begged as a personal favour for an individual examination of the family and servants on their opinion. The master was reluctant thus, as he expressed it, to go a-fooling, but his brother backed the Doctor up, and further prevented a general assembly to put one another to shame, but insisted on the witnesses being called in one by one. Oliver, the first summoned, was beginning to be somewhat less overawed by his father than in his earlier boyhood. To the inquiry what he thought of his brother Peregrine, he made a tentative sort of reply, that he was a strange fellow, who never could keep out of disgrace.

'That is not the question,' said his father. 'I am almost ashamed to speak it! Do you —nay, have you ever supposed him to be a——' he really could not bring out the word.

'A changeling, sir?' returned Oliver. 'I do not believe so now, knowing that it is impossible, but as a child I always did.'

'Who durst possess you with so foolish and profane a falsehood?'

'Every one, sir. I cannot recollect the time when I did not as entirely deem Peregrine a changeling elf as that Robin was my own brother. He believes so himself.'

'You have never striven to disabuse him.'

'Indeed, sir, he would scarce have listened to me had I done so; besides, to tell the truth, it has only been of late, since I have been older, and have studied more, that I have come to perceive the folly of it.'

Major Oakshott groaned, and bade him call Robert without saying wherefore. The little fellow came in, somewhat frightened, and when asked the question that had been put to his elder, his face lighted up, and he exclaimed, 'Oh, have they brought him back again?'

'Whom?'

'Our real brother, sir, who was carried off to fairyland!'

'Who told you so, Robert?'

He looked puzzled, and said, 'Sir, they all know it. Molly Owens, that was his foster-mother, saw the fairies bear him off on a broomstick up the chimney.'

'Robert, no lying!'

The boy was only restrained from tears by fear of his father, and just managed to say, ''Tis what they all say, and Perry knows.'

'Knows!' muttered Major Oakshott in despair, but the uncle, drawing Robin towards him, extracted that Perry had been seen flying out of the loft window, when he had been locked up—Robin had never seen it himself, but the maids had often done so. Moreover, there was proof positive, in the mark on Oliver's head, where he had nearly killed himself by tumbling downstairs, being lured by the fairies while they stole away the babe.

The Major could not listen with patience. 'A boy of that age to repeat such blasphemous nonsense!' he exclaimed; and Robert, restraining with difficulty his sobs of terror, was dismissed to fetch the butler.

The old Ironside who now appeared would not avouch his own disbelief in the identity of Master Peregrine, being, as he said, a man who had studied his Bible, listened to godly preachers, and seen the world; but he had no hesitation in declaring that almost every other soul in the household believed in it as firmly as in the Gospel, certainly all the women, and probably all the men, nor was there any doubt that the young gentleman conducted himself more like a goblin than the son of pious Christian parents. In effect both the clergyman and the Diplomate could not help suspecting that in other company the worthy butler's disavowal of all share in the superstition might have been less absolute.

'After this,' said Major Oakshott with a sigh, 'it seems useless to carry the inquiry farther.'

'What says my sister Oakshott?' inquired Sir Peregrine.

'She! Poor soul, she is too feeble to be fretted,' said her husband. 'She has never been the same woman since the Fire of London, and it would be vain to vex her with questions. She would be of one mind while I spoke to her, and another while her women were pouring their tales into her ear. Methinks I now understand why she has always seemed to shrink from this unfortunate child, and to fear rather than love him.'

'Even so, sir,' added the tutor. 'Much is explained that I never before understood. The question is how to deal with him under this fresh light. I will, so please your honour, assemble the family this very night, and expound to them that such superstitions are contrary to the very word of Scripture.'

'Much good will that do,' muttered the knight.

'I should humbly suggest, put in Dr. Woodford, 'that the best hope for the poor lad would be to place him where these foolish tales were unknown, and he could start afresh on the same terms with other youths.'

'There is no school in accordance with my principles,' said the Squire gloomily. 'Godly men who hold the faith as I do are inhibited by the powers that be from teaching in schools.'

'And,' said his brother, 'you hold these principles as more important than the causing your son to be bred up a human being instead of being pointed at and rendered hopeless as a demon.'

'I am bound to do so,' said the Major.

'Surely,' said Dr. Woodford, 'some scholar might be found, either here or in Holland, who might share your opinions, and could receive the boy without incurring penalties for opening a school without license.'

'It is a matter for prayer and consideration,' said Major Oakshott. 'Meantime, reverend sir, I thank you most heartily for the goodness with which you have treated my untoward son, and likewise for having opened my eyes to the root of his freakishness.'

The Doctor understood this as dismissal, and asked for his horse, intimating, however, that he would gladly keep the boy till some arrangement had been decided on. Then he rode home to tell his sister-in-law that he had done his best, and that he thought it a fortunate conjunction that the travelled brother had been present.

CHAPTER VI

A RELAPSE

'A tell-tale in their company
  They never could endure
And whoso kept not secretly
  Their pranks was punished sure.
It was a just and Christian deed
  To pinch such black and blue ;
Oh, how the commonwealth doth need
  Such justices as you !'
                          BISHOP CORBETT.

SEVERAL days passed, during which there could be no doubt that Peregrine Oakshott knew how to behave himself, not merely to grown-up people, but to little Anne, who had entirely lost her dread of him, and accepted him as a playfellow. He was able to join the family meals, and sit in the pleasant garden, shaded by the walls of the old castle, as well as by its own apple-trees, and looking out on the little bay in front, at full tide as smooth and shining as a lake.

There, while Anne did her task of spinning or of white seam, Mrs. Woodford would tell the children stories, or read to them from the *Pilgrim's Progress*, a wonderful romance to both. Peregrine, still tamed by weakness, would lie on the grass at her feet, in a tranquil bliss such as he had never known before, and his fairy romances to Anne were becoming mitigated, when one day a big coach came along the road from Fareham, with two boys riding beside it, escorting Lady Archfield and Mistress Lucy.

The lady was come to study Mrs. Woodford's recipe for preserved cherries, the young people, Charles, Lucy, and their cousin Sedley, now at home for the summer holidays, to spend an afternoon with Mistress Anne.

Great was Lady Archfield's surprise at finding that Major Oakshott's cross-grained slip of a boy was still at Portchester.

'If you were forced to take him in for very charity when he was hurt,' she said, 'I should have thought you would have been rid of him as soon as he could leave his bed.'

'The road to Oakwood is too rough for broken ribs as yet,' said Mrs. Woodford, 'nor is the poor boy ready for discipline.'

'Ay, I fancy that Major Oakshott is a bitter Puritan in his own house; but no discipline could be too harsh for such a boy as that, according to all that I hear,' said her ladyship, 'nor does he look as if much were amiss with him so far as may be judged of features so strange and writhen.'

'He is nearly well, but not yet strong, and we are keeping him here till his father has decided on what is best for him.'

'You even trust him with your little maid! And alone! I wonder at you, madam.'

'Indeed, my lady, I have seen no harm come of it. He is gentle and kind with Anne, and I think she softens him.'

Still Mrs. Woodford would gladly not have been bound to her colander and preserving-pan in her still-room, where her guest's housewifely mind found great scope for inquiry and comment, lasting for nearly two hours.

When at length the operations were over, and numerous little pots of jam tied up as specimens for the Archfield family to taste at home, the children were not in sight. No doubt, said Mrs. Woodford, they would be playing in the castle court, and the visitor accompanied her thither in some anxiety about broken walls and steps, but they were not in sight, nor did calls bring them.

The children had gone out together, Anne feeling altogether at ease and natural with congenial playmates. Even Sedley's tortures were preferable to Peregrine's attentions, since the first were only the tyranny of a graceless boy, the other gave her an indescribable sense of strangeness from which these ordinary mundane comrades were a relief and protection.

However, Charles and Sedley rushed off to see a young colt in which they were interested, and Lucy, in spite of her first shrinking, found Peregrine better company than she could have expected, when he assisted in swinging her and Anne by turns under the old ash-tree.

When the other two were seen approaching, the swinging girl hastily sprang out, only too well aware what Sedley's method of swinging would be. Then as the boys came up followed inquiries why Peregrine had not joined them, and jests in schoolboy taste ensued as to elf-locks in the horses' manes, and inquiries when he had last ridden to a witch's sabbath. Little Anne, in duty bound, made her protest, but this only incited Charles to add his word to the teasing, till Lucy joined in the laugh.

By and by, as they loitered along, they came to the Doctor's little boat, and there was a proposal to get in and rock. Lucy refused, out of respect for her company attire, and Anne could not leave her, so the two young ladies turned away with arms round each other's waists, Lucy demonstratively rejoicing to be quit of the troublesome boys.

Before they had gone far an eldritch shout of laughter was responded to by a burst of furious dismay and imprecation. The boat with the two boys was drifting out to sea, and Peregrine capering wildly on the shore, but in another instant he had vanished into the castle.

Anne had presence of mind enough to rush to the nearest fisherman's cottage, and send him out to bring them back, and it was at this juncture that the two mothers arrived on the scene. There was little real danger. A rope was thrown and caught, and after about half an hour of watching they were safely landed, but the tide had ebbed so far that they had to take off their shoes and stockings and wade through the mud. They were open-mouthed against the imp who had enticed them to rock in the boat, then in one second had cut the painter, bounded out, and sent them adrift with his mocking 'Ho! ho! ho!' Sedley Archfield clenched his fists, and gazed round wildly in search of the goblin to chastise him soundly, and Charles was ready to rush all over the castle in search of him.

'Two to one!' cried Anne, 'and he so small; you would never be so cowardly.'

'As if he were like an honest fellow,' said Charley. 'A goblin like that has his odds against a dozen of us.'

'I'd teach him, if I could but catch him,' cried Sedley.

'I told you,' said Anne, 'that he would be good if you would let him alone and not plague him.'

'Now, Anne,' said Charles, as he sat putting on his stockings, 'how could I stand being cast off for that hobgoblin, that looks as if he had been cut out of a root of yew with a blunt knife, and all crooked! I that always was your sweetheart, to see you consorting with a mis-shapen squinting Whig of a Nonconformist like that.'

'Nonconformist! I'll Nonconform him indeed,' added Sedley. 'I wish I had the wringing of his neck.'

'Now is not that hard!' said Anne; 'a poor lad who has been very sick, and that every one baits and spurns.'

'Serve him right,' said Sedley; 'he shall have more of the same sauce!'

'I think he has cast his spell on Anne,' added Charles, 'or how can she stand up for him?'

'My mamma bade me be kind to him.'

'Kind! I would as lief be kind to a toad!' put in Lucy.

'To see you kind to him makes me sick,'

exclaimed Charles. 'You see what comes of it.'

'It did not come of my kindness, but of your unkindness,' reasoned Anne.

'I told you so,' said Charles. 'You would have been best pleased if we had been carried out to sea and drowned!'

Anne burst into tears and disavowed any such intention, and Charles was protesting that he would only forgive her on condition of her never showing any kindness to Peregrine again, when a sudden shower of sand and pebbles descended, one of them hitting Sedley pretty sharply on the ear. The boys sprang up with a howl of imprecation and vengeance, but no one was to be seen, only 'Ho! ho! ho!' resounded from the battlements. Off they rushed headlong, but the nearest door was in a square tower a good way off, and when they reached it the door defied their efforts of frantic rage, whilst another shower descended on them from above, accompanied by the usual shout. But while they were dashing off in quest of another entrance they were met by a servant sent to summon them to return home. Coach and horses were at the door, and Lady Archfield was in haste to get them away, declaring that she should not think their lives safe near that fiendish monster. Considering that Sedley was nearly twice as big as Peregrine, and Charles a strong well-grown lad, this was a tribute to his preternatural powers.

Very unwillingly they went, and if Lady Archfield had not kept a strict watch from her coach window, they would certainly have turned back to revenge the pranks played on them. The last view of them showed Sedley turning round shaking his whip and clenching his teeth in defiance. Mrs. Woodford was greatly concerned, especially as Peregrine could not be found and did not appear at supper.

'Had he run away to sea?' the usual course of refractory lads at Portchester, but for so slight a creature only half recovered it did not seem probable. It was more likely that he had gone home, and that Mrs. Woodford felt as somewhat a mortifying idea. However, on looking into his chamber, as she sought her own, she beheld him in bed, with his face turned into the pillow, whether asleep or feigning slumber there was no knowing.

Later, she heard sounds that induced her to go and look at him. He was starting, moaning, and babbling in his sleep. But with morning all his old nature seemed to have returned.

There was a hedgehog in Anne's bowl of milk, Mrs. Woodford's poultry were cackling hysterically at an unfortunate kitten suspended from an apple-tree and let down and drawn up among them. The three-legged stool of the old waiting-woman 'toppled down headlong' as though by the hands of Puck, and even on Anne's arms certain black and blue marks of nails were discovered, and when her mother examined her on them she only cried and begged not to be made to answer.

And while Dr. Woodford was dozing in his chair as usual after the noonday dinner, Mrs. Woodford actually detected a hook suspended from a horsehair descending in the direction of his big horn spectacles, and quietly moving across to frustrate the attempt, she unearthed Peregrine on a chair angling from behind the window curtain.

She did not speak, but fixed her calm eyes

on him with a look of sad, grave disappointment as she wound up the line. In a few seconds the boy had thrown himself at her feet, rolling as if in pain, and sobbing out, ' 'Tis all of no use! Let me alone.'

Nevertheless he obeyed the hushing gesture of her hand, and held his breath, as she led him out to the garden-seat, where they had spent so many happy quiet hours. Then he flung himself down and repeated his exclamation, half piteous, half defiant. ' Leave me alone! Leave me alone! It has me! It is all of no use.'

' What has you, my poor child ? '

' The evil spirit. You will have it that I'm not one of—one of them—so it must be as my father says, that I am possessed—the evil spirit. I was at peace with you—so happy —happier than ever I was before—and now —those boys. It has me again—I could not help it—I've even hurt her—Mistress Anne. Let me alone—send me home—to be scorned, and shunned, and brow-beaten—and as bad as ever—then at least she will be safe from me.'

All this came out between sobs such that

Mrs. Woodford could not attempt to speak, but she kept her hand on him, and at last she said, when he could hear her: 'Every one of us has to fight with an evil spirit, and when we are not on our guard he is but too apt to take advantage of us.'

The boy rather sullenly repeated that it was of no use to fight against his.

'Indeed! Nay. Were you ever so much grieved before at having let him have the mastery?'

'No—but no one ever was good to me before.'

'Yes; all about you lived under a cruel error, and you helped them in it. But if you had not a better nature in you, my poor child, you would not be happy here and thankful for what we can do for you.'

'I was like some one else here,' said Peregrine, picking a daisy to pieces, 'but they stirred it all up. And at home I shall be just the same as ever I was.'

She longed to tell him that there was hope of a change in his life, but she durst not till it was more certain, so she said—

'There was One who came to conquer

the evil spirit and the evil nature, and to give each one of us the power to get the victory. The harder the victory, the more glorious!' and her eyes sparkled at the thought.

He caught a moment's glow, then fell back. 'For those that are chosen,' he said.

'You are chosen—you were chosen by your baptism. You have the stirrings of good within you. You can win and beat back the evil side of you in Christ's strength, if you will ask for it, and go on in His might.'

The boy groaned. Mrs. Woodford knew that the great point with him would be to teach him to hope and to pray, but the very name of prayer had been rendered so distasteful to him that she scarce durst press the subject by name, and her heart sank at the thought of sending him home again, but she was glad to be interrupted, and said no more.

At night, however, she heard sounds of moaning and stifled babbling that reminded her of his times of delirium, and going into his room she found him tossing and groaning so that it was manifestly a kindness to wake him; but her gentle touch occasioned a scream of terror, and he started aside with open glassy eyes, crying, 'Oh take me not!'

'My dear boy! It is I. Perry, do you not know me?'

'Oh, madam!' in infinite relief, 'it is you. I thought—I thought I was in elf-land and that they were paying me for the tithe to hell;' and he still shuddered all over.

'No elf—no elf, dear boy; a christened boy—God's child, and under His care;' and she began the 121st Psalm.

'Oh, but I am not under His shadow! The Evil One has had me again! He will have me. Aren't those his claws? He will have me!'

'Never, my child, if you will cry to God for help. Say this with me, " Lord, be Thou my keeper."'

He did so, and grew more quiet, and she began to repeat Dr. Ken's evening hymn, which had become known in manuscript in Winchester. It soothed him, and she thought he was dropping off to sleep, but no sooner did she move than he started with 'There it is again—the black wings—the claws—' then while awake, 'Say it again! Oh, say it again. Fold me in your prayers—you can pray.' She went back to the verse, and he became quiet, but her next attempt to leave him caused an entreaty that she would remain, nor could she quit him till the dawn, happily very early, was dispelling the terrors of the night, and then, when he had himself murmured once—

> 'Let no ill dreams disturb my rest,
> No powers of darkness me molest,'

he fell asleep at last, with a softer look on his pinched face. Poor boy, would that verse be his first step to prayer and deliverance from his own too real enemy?

CHAPTER VII

THE ENVOY

'I then did ask of her, her changeling child.'
Midsummer Night's Dream.

Mrs. Woodford was too good a housewife to allow herself any extra rest on account of her vigil, and she had just put her Juneating apple-tart into the oven when Anne rushed into the kitchen with the warning that there was a grand gentleman getting off his horse at the gateway, and speaking to her uncle—she thought it must be Peregrine's uncle.

Mrs. Woodford was of the same opinion, and asked where Peregrine was.

'Fast asleep in the window-seat of the parlour, mother! I did not waken him, for he looked so tired.'

'That was right, my little maiden,' said Mrs. Woodford, hastily washing her hands, taking off her cooking apron, letting down her black gown from its pocket holes, and arranging her veil-like widow's coif, after which, in full trim for company, she sallied out to the front door, to avert, if possible, the wakening of the boy, whom she wished to appear to the best advantage.

She met in the garden her brother-in-law, and Sir Peregrine Oakshott, on being presented to her, made such a bow as had seldom been seen in those parts, as he politely said that he was the bearer of his brother's thanks for her care of his nephew.

Mrs. Woodford explained that the boy had had so bad a night that it would be well not to break his present sleep, and invited the guest to walk in the garden or sit in the Doctor's study or in the shade of the castle wall.

This last was what he preferred, and there they seated themselves, with a green slope before them down to the pale gray creek, and the hill beyond lying in the summer sunshine.

'I have been long in coming hither,' said the knight, 'partly on account of letters on affairs of State, and partly likewise because I desired to come alone, thinking that I might better understand how it is with the lad without the presence of his father or brothers.'

'I am very glad you have done so, sir.'

'Then, madam, I entreat of you to speak freely and tell me your opinion of him without reserve. You need not fear offence by speaking of the mode in which they have treated him at home. My poor brother has meant to do his duty, but he has stood so far aloof from his sons that he has dealt with them in ignorance, and their mother, between sickliness and timidity, is a mere prey to the folly of her gossips. So speak plainly, madam, I beg of you.'

Mrs. Woodford did speak plainly of the boy's rooted belief in his own elfish origin, and how when arguing against it she had found the alternative even sadder and more hopeless, how well he comported himself as long as he was treated as a human and rational being, but how the taunts and jests of the young Archfields had renewed all the mischief, to the poor fellow's own remorse and despair.

Sir Peregrine listened with only a word of

comment, or question now and then, like a man of the world well used to hearing all before he committed himself, and the description was only just ended when the clang of the warning dinner-bell sounded and they rose; but as they were passing the window of the dining-parlour a shriek of Anne's startled them all, and as they sprang forward, Mrs. Woodford first, Peregrine's voice was heard, 'No, no, Anne, don't be afraid. It is for me he is come; I knew he would.'

Something in a strange language was heard. A black face with round eyes and gleaming teeth might be seen bending forward. Anne gave another shriek, but was heard crying, 'No, no! Get away, sir. He is our Lord Christ's! He is! You can't! you shan't have him.'

And Anne was seen standing over Peregrine, who had dropped shuddering and nearly fainting on the floor, while she stood valiantly up warding off the advance of him whom she took for the Prince of Darkness, and in her excitement not at first aware of those who were come to her aid at the window. In one second the negro was saying something which his master answered, and sent him off. Mrs. Woodford had called out, 'Don't be afraid, dear children. 'Tis Sir Peregrine's black servant'; and the Doctor, 'Foolish children! What is this nonsense?' A moment or two more and they were in the room, Anne, all trembling, flying up to her mother and hiding her face against her between fright and shame at not having thought of the black servant, and the while they lifted up Peregrine, who, as he met his kind friend's eyes, said faintly, 'Is he gone? was it the dream again?'

'It was your uncle's blackamoor servant,' said Mrs. Woodford. 'You woke up, and no wonder you were startled. Come with me, both of you, and make you ready for dinner.'

Peregrine had rather collapsed than fainted, for he was able to walk with her hand on his shoulder, and Sir Peregrine understood her sign and did not attempt to accost either of the children, though as the Doctor took him to his chamber he expressed his admiration of the little maiden.

'That's the right woman,' he said, 'losing herself when there is one to guard. Nay, sir, she needs no excuse. Such a spirit may well redeem a child's mistake.'

Mrs. Woodford had reassured the children, so that they were more than half ashamed, though scarce willing to reappear when she had made Peregrine wash his face and hands, smooth the hair ruffled in his nap, freshly tying his little cravat and the ribbons on his shoes and at his knees. To make his hair into anything but elf locks, or to obliterate the bristly tuft that made him like Riquet, was impossible, illness had made him additionally lean and sallow, and his keen eyes, under their black contracted brows and dark lashes, showed all the more the curious variation in their tints, and with an obliquity that varied according to the state of the nerves. There was a satirical mischievous cast in the mould of the face, though individually the features were not amiss except for their thinness, and in fact the unpleasantness of the expression had insensibly been softened during this last month, and there was nothing repellant, though much that was quaint, in the slight figure, with the indescribably one-sided air, and stature more befitting ten than fourteen years. What would the visitor think of him? The Doctor called to him, 'Come, Peregrine, your uncle, Sir Peregrine Oakshott, has been good enough to come over to see you.'

Peregrine had been well trained enough in that bitter school of home to make a correct bow, though his feelings were betrayed by his yellow eye going almost out of sight.

'My namesake—your father will not let me say my godson,' said Sir Peregrine smiling. 'We ought to be good friends.'

The boy looked up. Perhaps he had never been greeted in so human a manner before, and there was something confiding in the way those bony fingers of his rested a moment in his uncle's clasp.

'And this is your little daughter, madam, Peregrine's kind playmate? You may well be proud of her valour,' said the knight, while Anne made her courtesy, which he, in the custom of the day, returned with a kiss; and she, who had been mortally ashamed of her terror, marvelled at his praise.

The pair of fowls were by this time on the table, and good manners required silence on the part of the children, but while Sir Peregrine explained that he had been appointed by his Majesty as Envoy to the Elector of Brandenburg, and gave various interesting particulars of foreign life, Mrs. Woodford saw that he was keeping a quiet watch over his nephew's habits at table, and she was thankful that when unmoved by any wayward spirit of mischief they were quite beyond reproach. Something of the refinement of his poor mother's tastes must have been inherited by Peregrine, for a certain daintiness of taste and habit had probably added to his discomforts in the austere, not to say rude simplicity imposed upon the children of the family.

When the meal was over the children were dismissed to the garden, but bidden to keep within call, in case Sir Peregrine should wish to see his nephew again. The others repaired again to the garden seat, with wine and fruit, but the knight begged Mrs. Woodford not to leave them.

'I am satisfied,' he said. 'The boy shows gentle blood and breeding. There was cause enough for fright without cowardice, and there is not, what I was lead to fear, such uncouthness or ungainliness as should hinder me from having him with me.'

'Oh, sir, is that your purpose?' cried the lady, almost as eagerly as if it had been high preferment for her own child.

'I had thought thereon,' said the envoy. 'There is reason that he should be my charge, and my brother is like to give a ready consent, since he is sorely perplexed what to do with this poor untoward slip.'

'He would be less untoward were he happier,' said Mrs. Woodford. 'Indeed, sir, I do not think you will repent it, if——' and she paused.

'What would you say, madam?'

'If only all your honour's household are absolutely ignorant of all these tales.'

'That can well be, madam. I have only one body-servant with me, this unlucky black-amoor, who speaks nothing save Dutch. I had already thought of leaving my grooms here, and returning to London by sea, and this could well be done, and would cut off all channels of gossiping. The boy is, the chaplain tells me, quick-witted, and a fair scholar for his years, and I can find good schooling for him.'

'When his head is able to bear it,' said Mrs. Woodford.

'Truly, sir,' added the Doctor, 'you are doing a good work, and I trust that the boy will requite you worthily.'

'I tell your reverence,' said Sir Peregrine, 'crooked stick though they term him, I had ten times rather have the dealing with him than with those comely great lubbers his brothers! The question now is, shall I tell him what is in store for him?'

'I should say,' returned Dr. Woodford, 'that provided it is certain that the intention can be carried out, nothing would be so good for him as hope. Do you not say so, sister?'

'Indeed I do,' she replied. 'I believe that he would be a very different boy if he were relieved from the misery he suffers at home and requites by mischievous pranks. I do not say he will or can be a good lad at once, but if your honour can have patience with him, I do believe there is that in him which can be turned to good. If he only can believe in the better nature and higher guidings, and pray, and not give himself up in despair.' She had tears in her eyes.

'My good madam, I can believe it all,' said Sir Peregrine. 'Short of being supposed an elf, I have gone through the same, and it was not my good father's fault that I did not loathe the very name of preaching or prayer. But I had a mother who knew how to deal with me, whereas this poor child's mother, I am sure, believes in her secret heart that he is none of hers, though she has enough sense not to dare to avow it. Alas! I cannot give the boy the woman's tending by which you have already wrought so much,' and Mrs. Woodford remembered to have heard that his wife had died at Rotterdam, 'but I can treat him like a human being, I hope indeed as a son; and, at any rate, there will be no one to remind him of these old wives' tales.'

'I can only say that I am heartily rejoiced,' said Mrs. Woodford.

So Peregrine was summoned, and shambled up, his eyes showing that he expected a trying interview, and, moreover, with a certain twinkle of mischief or perverseness in their corners.

'Soh! my lad, we ought to be better acquainted,' said the uncle. 'D'ye know what our name means?'

'*Peregrinus*, a vagabond,' responded the boy.

'Eh! The translation may be correct, but 'tis scarce the most complimentary. I wonder now if you, like me, were born on a Wednesday. "Wednesday's child has far to go."'

'No. I was born on a Sunday, and if to see goblins and oafs——'

'Nay, I read it, "Sunday's child is full of grace."'

Peregrine's mouth twitched ironically, but his uncle continued, 'Look you, my boy, what say you to fulfilling the augury of your name with me. His Majesty has ordered me off again to represent the British name to the Elector of Brandenburg, and I have a mind to carry you with me. What do you say?'

If any one expected Peregrine to be overjoyed his demeanour was disappointing. He shuffled with his feet, and after two or three

'Ehs?' from his uncle, he mumbled, ' I don't care,' and then shrank together, as one prepared for the stripe with the riding-whip which such a rude answer merited: but his uncle had, as a diplomate, learnt a good deal of patience, and he said, ' Ha! don't care to leave home and brothers. Eh?'

Peregrine's chin went down, and there was no answer; his hair dropped over his heavy brow.

'See, boy, this is no jest,' said his uncle. 'You are too big to be told that "I'll put you into my pocket and carry you off." I am in earnest.'

Peregrine looked up, and with one sudden flash surveyed his uncle. His lips trembled, but he did not speak.

'It is sudden,' said the knight to the other two. 'See, boy, I am not about to take you away with me now. In a week or ten days' time I start for London; and there we will fit you out for Königsberg or Berlin, and I trust we shall make a man of you, and a good man. Your tutor tells me you have excellent parts, and I mean that you shall do me credit.'

Dr. Woodford could not help telling the lad that he ought to thank his uncle, whereat he scowled; but Sir Peregrine said, 'He is not ready for that yet. Wait till he feels he has something to thank me for.'

So Peregrine was dismissed, and his friends exclaimed with some wonder and annoyance that the boy who had been willing to be decapitated to put an end to his wretchedness, should be so reluctant to accept such an offer, but Sir Peregrine only laughed, and said—

'The lad has pith in him! I like him better than if he came like a spaniel to my foot. But I will say no more till I fully have my brother's consent. No one knows what crooks there may be in folk's minds.'

He took his leave, and presently Mrs. Woodford had a fresh surprise. She found this strange boy lying flat on the grass, sobbing as if his heart would break, and when she tried to soothe and comfort him it was very hard to get a word from him; but at last, as she asked, 'And does it grieve you so much to leave home?' the answer was—

'No, no! not home!'

'What is it, then? What are you sorry to leave?'

'Oh, *you* don't know! you and Anne—the only ones that ever were good to me—and drove away—*it.*'

'Nay, my dear boy. Your uncle means to be good to you.'

'No, no. No one ever will be like you and Anne. Oh, let me stay with you, or they will have me at last!'

He was too much shaken, in his still half-recovered state, by the events of these last days, to be reasoned with. Mrs. Woodford was afraid he would work himself into delirium, and could only soothe him into a calmer state. She found from Anne that the children had some vague hopes of his being allowed to remain at Portchester, and that this was the ground of his disappointment, since he seemed to be attaching himself to them as the first who had ever touched his heart or opened to him a gleam of better things.

By the next day, however, he was in a quieter and more reasonable state, and Mrs. Woodford was able to have a long talk with him. She represented that the difference of opinions made it almost certain that his father would never consent to his remaining under her roof, and that even if this were possible, Portchester was far too much infected with the folly from which he had suffered so much; and his uncle would take care that no one he would meet should ever hear of it.

'There's little good in that,' said the boy moodily. 'I'm a thing they'll jibe at and bait any way,'

'I do not see that, if you take pains with yourself. Your uncle said you showed blood and breeding, and when you are better dressed, and with him, no one will dare to mock his Excellency's nephew. Depend upon it, Peregrine, this is the fresh start that you need.'

'If you were there——'

'My boy, you must not ask for what is impossible. You must learn to conquer in God's strength, not mine.'

All, however, that passed may not here be narrated, and it apparently left that wayward spirit unconvinced. Nevertheless, when on the second day Major Oakshott himself came over with his brother, and informed Peregrine that his uncle was good enough to undertake the charge of him, and to see that he was bred up in godly ways in a Protestant land, free from prelacy and superstition, the boy seemed reconciled to his fate. Major Oakshott spoke more kindly than usual to him, being free from fresh irritation at his misdemeanours; but even thus there was a contrast with the gentler, more persuasive tones of the diplomatist, and no doubt this tended to increase Peregrine's willingness to be thus handed over.

The next question was whether he should go home first, but both the uncle and the friends were averse to his remaining there, amid the unavoidable gossip and chatter of the household, and it was therefore decided that he should only ride over with Dr. Woodford for an hour or two to take leave of his mother and brothers.

This settled, Mrs. Woodford found him much easier to deal with. He had really, through his midnight invocation of the fairies, obtained an opening into a new world, and he was ready to believe that with no one to twit him with being a changeling or worse, he could avoid perpetual disgrace and punishment and live at peace. Nor was he unwilling to promise Mrs. Woodford to say daily, and especially when tempted, one or two brief collects and ejaculations which she selected to teach him, as being as unlike as possible to the long extempore exercises which had made him hate the very name of prayer. The Doctor gave him a Greek Testament, as being least connected with unpleasant recollections.

'And,' entreated Peregrine humbly, in a low voice to Mrs. Woodford on his last Sunday evening, 'may I not have something of yours, to lay hold of, and remember you if—when—the evil spirit tries to lay hold of me again?'

She would fain have given him a prayer-book, but she knew that would be treason to his father, and with tears in her eyes and something of a pang, she gave him a tiny miniature of herself, which had been her husband's companion at sea, and hung it round his neck with the chain of her own hair that had always held it.

'It will always keep my heart warm,' said
Peregrine, as he hid it under his vest. There
was a shade of disappointment on Anne's face
when he showed it to her, for she had almost
deemed it her own.

'Never mind, Anne,' he said; 'I'm coming back a knight like my uncle to marry you,
and then it will be yours again.'

'I—I'm not going to wed you—I have
another sweetheart,' added Anne in haste,
lest he should think she scorned him.

'Oh, that lubberly Charles Archfield! No
fear of him. He is promised long ago to some
little babe of quality in London. You may
whistle for him. So you'd better wait for me.'

'It is not true. You only say it to plague
me.'

'It's as true as Gospel! I heard Sir
Philip telling one of the big black gowns one
day in the Close, when I was sitting up in a
tree overhead, how they had fixed a marriage
between his son and his old friend's daughter,
who would have ever so many estates. So
I'd give that'—snapping his fingers—'for
your chances of being my Lady Archfield in
the salt mud at Fareham.'

'I shall ask Lucy. It is not kind of you, Perry, when you are just going away.'

'Come, come, don't cry, Anne.'

'But I knew Charley ever so long first, and——'

'Oh yes. Maids always like straight, comely, dull fellows, I know that. But as you can't have Charles Archfield, I mean to have you, Anne—for I shall look to you as the only one as can ever make a good man of me! Ay—your mother—I'd wed her if I could, but as I can't, I mean to have you, Anne Woodford.'

'I don't mean to have you! I shall go to Court, and marry some noble earl or gentleman! Why do you laugh and make that face, Peregrine? you know my father was almost a knight——'

'Nobody is long with you without knowing that!' retorted Peregrine; 'but a miss is as good as a mile, and you will find the earls and the lords will think so, and be fain to take the crooked stick at last!'

Mistress Anne tossed her head—and Peregrine returned a grimace. Nevertheless they parted with a kiss, and for some time the thought of Peregrine haunted the little girl with a strange, fateful feeling, between aversion and attraction, which wore off, as a folly of her childhood, with her growth in years.

CHAPTER VIII

THE RETURN

'I think he bought his doublet in Italy, his round hose in France, his bonnet in Germany, and his behaviour everywhere.'—Merchant of Venice.

It was autumn, but in the year 1687, when again Lucy Archfield and Anne Jacobina Woodford were pacing the broad gravel walk along the south side of the nave of Winchester Cathedral. Lucy, in spite of her brocade skirt and handsome gown of blue velvet tucked up over it, was still devoid of any look of distinction, but was a round-faced, blooming, cheerful maiden, of that ladylike thoroughly countrified type happily frequent in English girlhood throughout all time.

Anne, or Jacobina, as she tried to be called, towered above her head, and had never lost that tincture of courtly grace that early breeding had given her, and though her skirt was of gray wool, and the upper gown of cherry tabinet, she wore both with an air that made them seem more choice and stylish than those of her companion, while the simple braids and curls of her brown hair set off an unusually handsome face, pale and clear in complexion, with regular features, fine arched eyebrows over clear brown eyes, a short chin, and a mouth of perfect outline, but capable of looking very resolute.

Altogether she looked fit for a Court atmosphere, and perhaps she was not without hopes of it, for Dr. Woodford had become a royal chaplain under Charles II, and was now continued in the same office; and though this was a sinecure as regarded the present King, yet Tory and High Church views were as much in the ascendant as they could be under a Romanist king, and there were hopes of a canonry at Windsor or Westminster, or even higher preferment still, if he were not reckoned too staunch an Anglican. That Mrs. Woodford's health had been failing for many months past would, her sanguine daughter thought, be remedied by being nearer the best physicians in London, which had been quitted with regret. Meantime Lucy's first experiences of wedding festivities were to be heard. For the Archfield family had just returned from celebrating the marriage of the heir. Long ago Anne Jacobina had learnt to reckon Master Charles's pledges of affection among the sports and follies of childhood, and the strange sense of disappointment and shame with which she recollected them had perhaps added to her natural reserve, and made her feel it due to maidenly dignity to listen with zest to the account of the bride, who was to be brought to supper at Dr. Woodford's that eve.

'She is a pretty little thing,' said Lucy; 'but my mother was much concerned to find her so mere a child, and would not, if she had seen her, have consented to the marriage for two years to come, except for the sake of having her in our own hands.'

'I thought she was sixteen.'

'Barely fifteen, my dear, and far younger than we were at that age. She cried because her woman said she must leave her old doll behind her; and when my brother declared that she should have anything she liked, she danced about, and kissed him, and made him kiss its wooden face with half the paint rubbed off.'

'He did?'

'Oh yes! She is like a pretty fresh plaything to him, and they go about together just like big Towzer and little Frisk at home. He is very much amused with her, and she thinks him the finest possession that ever came in her way.'

'Well, so he is.'

'That is true; but somehow it is scarcely like husband and wife; and my mother fears that she may be sickly, for she is so small and slight that it seems as if you could blow her away, and so white that you would think she had no blood, except when a little heat brings the purest rose colour to her cheek, and that, my lady says, betokens weakliness. You know, of course, that she is an orphan; her father died of a wasting consumption, and her mother not long after, when she was a yearling babe. It was her grandfather who was my father's friend in the old cavalier days, and wrote to propose the contract to my brother not long before his death, when she was but five years old. The pity was that she was not sent to us at once, for the old lord, her grand-uncle, never heeded or cared for her, but left her to servants, who petted her, but understood nothing of care of her health or her education, so that the only wonder is that she is alive or so sweet and winning as she is. She can hardly read without spelling, and I had to make copies for her of Alice Fitzhubert, to show her how to sign the book. All she knew she learnt from the old steward, and only when she liked. My father laughs and is amused, but my lady sighs, and hopes her portion is not dearly bought.'

'Is not she to be a great heiress?'

'Not of the bulk of the lands—they go to heirs male; but there is much besides, enough to make Charles a richer man than our father. I wonder what you will think of her. My mother is longing to talk her over with Mrs. Woodford.'

'And my mother is longing to see my lady.'

'I fear she is still but poorly.'

'We think she will be much better when we get home,' said Anne. 'I am sure she is stronger, for she walked round the Close yesterday, and was scarcely tired.'

'But tell me, Anne, is it true that poor Master Oliver Oakshott is dead of small-pox?'

'Quite true. Poor young gentleman, he was to have married that cousin of his mother's, Mistress Martha Browning, living at Emsworth. She came on a visit, and they think she brought the infection, for she sickened at once, and though she had it favourably, is much disfigured. Master Oliver caught it and died in three days, and all the house were down with it. They say poor Mrs. Oakshott forgot her ailments and went to and fro among them all. My mother would have gone to help in their need if she had been as well as she used to be.'

'How is it with the other son? He was a personable youth enough. I saw him at the ship launch in the spring, and thought both lads would fain have staid for the dance on board but for their grim old father.'

'You saw Robert, but he is not the elder.'

'What? Is that shocking impish urchin whom we used to call Riquet with the tuft, older than he?'

'Certainly he is. He writes from time to time to my mother, and seems to be doing well with his uncle.'

'I cannot believe he would come to good. Do you remember his sending my brother and cousin adrift in the boat?'

'I think that was in great part the fault of your cousin for mocking and tormenting him.'

'Sedley Archfield was a bad boy! There's no denying that. I am afraid he had good reason for running away from college.'

'Have you heard of him since?'

'Yes; he has been serving with the Life-guards in Scotland, and mayhap he will come home and see us. My father wishes to see whether he is worthy to have a troop procured by money or favour for him, and if they are recalled to the camp at November it will be an opportunity. But see—who is coming through the Slype?'

'My uncle. And who is with him?'

Dr. Woodford advanced, and with him a

small slender figure in black. As the broad hat with sable plume was doffed with a sweep on approaching the ladies, a dark head and peculiar countenance appeared, while the Doctor said, 'Here is an old acquaintance, young ladies, whom I met dismounting at the White Hart, and have brought home with me.'

'Mr. Peregrine Oakshott!' exclaimed Anne, feeling bound to offer in welcome a hand, which he kissed after the custom of the day, while Lucy dropped a low and formal courtesy, and being already close to the gate of the house occupied by her family, took her leave till supper-time.

Even in the few steps before reaching home Anne was able to perceive that a being very unlike the imp of seven years ago had returned, though still short in stature and very slight, with long dark hair hanging straight enough to suggest elf-locks, but his figure was well proportioned, and had a finished air of high breeding and training. His riding suit was point device, from the ostrich feather in his hat, to the toes of his well-made boots, and his sword knew its place, as well as did those of the gentlemen that Anne remembered at the Duke of York's when she was a little child. His thin, marked face was the reverse of handsome, but it was keen, shrewd, perhaps satirical, and the remarkable eyes were very bright under dark eyebrows and lashes, and the thin lips, devoid of hair, showed fine white teeth when parted by a smile of gladness — at the meeting — though he was concerned to hear that Mrs. Woodford had been very ill all the last spring, and had by no means regained her former health, and even in the few words that passed it might be gathered that Anne was far more hopeful than her uncle.

She did indeed look greatly changed, though her countenance was sweeter than ever, as she rose from her seat by the fire and held out her arms to receive the newcomer with a motherly embrace, while the expression of joy and affection was such as could never once have seemed likely to sit on Peregrine Oakshott's features. They were left together, for Anne had the final touches to put to the supper, and Dr. Woodford was sent for to speak to one of the Cathedral staff.

Peregrine explained that he was on his way home, his father having recalled him on his brother's death, but he hoped soon to rejoin his uncle, whose secretary he now was. They had been for the last few months in London, and were thence to be sent on an embassy to the young Czar of Muscovy, an expedition to which he looked forward with eager curiosity. Mrs. Woodford hoped that all danger of infection at Oakwood was at an end.

'There is none for me, madam,' he said, with a curious writhed smile. 'Did you not know that they thought they were rid of me when I took the disease at seven years old, and lay in the loft over the hen-house with Molly Owens to tend me? and I believe it was thought to be fairy work that I came out of it no more unsightly than before.'

'You are seeking for compliments, Peregrine; you are greatly improved.'

'Crooked sticks can be pruned and trained,' he responded, with a courteous bow.

'You are a travelled man. Let me see, how many countries have you seen?'

'A year at Berlin and Königsberg—strange places enough, specially the last, two among the scholars and high roofs of Leyden, half a year at Versailles and Paris, another year at Turin, whence back for another half year to wait on old King Louis, then to the Hague, and the last three months at Court. Not much like buying and selling cows, or growing wheat on the slopes, or lying out on a cold winter's night to shoot a few wild fowl; and I have you to thank for it, my first and best friend!'

'Nay, your uncle is surely your best.'

'Never would he have picked up the poor crooked stick save for you, madam. Moreover, you gave me my talisman,' and he laid his hand on his breast; 'it is your face that speaks to me and calls me back when the elf, or whatever it is, has got the mastery of me.'

Somewhat startled, Mrs. Woodford would have asked what he meant, but that intelligence was brought that Mr. Oakshott's man had brought his mail, so that he had to repair to his room. Mrs. Woodford had kept up some correspondence with him, for which his uncle's position as envoy afforded unusual facilities, and she knew that on the whole he had been a very different being from what he was at home. Once, indeed, his uncle had written to the Doctor to express his full satisfaction in the lad, on whom he seemed to look like a son, but from some subsequent letters she had an impression that he had got into trouble of some sort while at the University of Leyden, and she was afraid that she must accept the belief that the wild elfish spirit, as he called it, was by no means extinct in him, any more, she said to herself, than temptation is in any human creature. The question is, What is there to contend therewith?

The guests were, however, about to assemble. The Doctor, in black velvet cap and stately silken cassock, sash, and gown, sailed down to receive them, and again greeted Peregrine, who emerged in black velvet and satin, delicate muslin cravat and cuffs, dainty silk stockings and rosetted shoes, in a style such as made the far taller and

handsomer Charles Archfield, in spite of gay
scarlet coat, embroidered flowery vest, rich
laced cravat, and thick shining brown curls,
look a mere big schoolboy, almost bumpkin-
like in contrast. However, no one did look
at anything but the little creature who could
just reach to hang upon that resplendent
bridegroom's arm. She was in glistening
white brocade, too stiff and cumbrous for so
tiny a figure, yet together with the diamonds
glistening on her head and breast giving her
the likeness of a fairy queen. The whiteness
was almost startling, for the neck and arms
were like pearl in tint, the hair flowing in
full curls on her shoulders was like shining
flax or pale silk just unwound from the
cocoon, and the only relief of colour was the
deep blue of the eyes, the delicate tint of the
lips, and the tender rosy flush that was called
up by her presentation to her hosts by stout
old Sir Philip, in plum-coloured coat and full-
bottomed wig, though she did not blush half
as much as the husband of nineteen in his
new character. Indeed, had it not been for
her childish prettiness, her giggle would have
been unpleasing to more than Lady Arch-

field, who, broad and matronly, gave a courtesy
and critical glance at Peregrine before subsid-
ing into a seat beside Mrs. Woodford.

Lucy stood among a few other young
people from the Close, watching for Anne,
who came in, trim and bright, though still
somewhat reddened in face and arms from
her last attentions to the supper—an elaborate
meal on such occasions, though lighter than
the mid-day repast. There were standing
pies of game, lobster and oyster patties,
creams, jellies, and other confections, on
which Sir Philip and his lady highly complimented Anne, who had been engaged on them
for at least a couple of days, her mother being
no longer able to assist except by advice.

'See, daughter Alice, you will learn one
day to build up a jelly as well as to eat it,'
said Sir Philip good-humouredly, whereat the
small lady pouted a little and said—

'Bet lets me make shapes of the dough,
but I won't stir the pans and get to look like
a turkey-cock.'

'Ah, ha! and you have always done what
you liked, my little madam?'

'Of course, sir! and so I shall,' she

answered, drawing up her pretty little head, while Lady Archfield gave hers a boding shake.

'Time, and life, and wifehood teach lessons,' murmured Mrs. Woodford in consolation, and the Doctor changed the subject by asking Peregrine whether the ladies abroad were given to housewifery.

'The German dames make a great ado about their *Wirthschaft*, as they call it,' was the reply, 'but as to the result! Pah! I know not how we should have fared had not Hans, my uncle's black, been an excellent cook; but it was in Paris that we were exquisitely regaled, and our *maître d'hôtel* would discourse on *ragoûts* and *entremets* till one felt as if his were the first of the sciences.'

'So it is to a Frenchman,' growled Sir Philip. 'French and Frenchifications are all the rage nowadays, but what will your father say to your science, my young spark?'

The gesture of head and shoulder that replied had certainly been caught at Paris. Mrs. Woodford rushed into the breach, asking about the Princess of Orange, whom she had often seen as a child.

'A stately and sightly dame is she, madam,' Peregrine answered, 'towering high above her little mynheer, who outwardly excels her in naught save the length of nose, and has the manners of a boor.'

'The Prince of Orange is the hope of the country,' said Sir Philip severely.

Peregrine's face wore a queer satirical look, which provoked Sir Philip into saying, 'Speak up, sir! what d'ye mean? We don't understand French grins here.'

'Nor does he, nor French courtesies either,' said Peregrine.

'So much the better!' exclaimed the baronet.

Here the little clear voice broke in, 'O Mr. Oakshott, if I had but known you were coming, you might have brought me a French doll in the latest fashion.'

'I should have been most happy, madam,' returned Peregrine; 'but unfortunately I am six months from Paris, and besides, his honour might object lest a French doll should contaminate the Dutch puppets.'

'But oh, sir, is it true that French dolls have real hair that will curl?'

'Don't be foolish,' muttered Charles impatiently; and she drew up her head and made an indescribably droll *moue* of disgust at him.

Supper ended, the party broke up into old and young, the two elder gentlemen sadly discussing politics over their tall glasses of wine, the matrons talking over the wedding and Lady Archfield's stay in London at the parlour fire, and the young folk in a window, waiting for the fiddler and a few more of the young people who were to join them in the dance.

The Archfield ladies had kissed the hand of the Queen, and agreed with Peregrine in admiration of her beauty and grace, though they did not go so far as he did, especially when he declared that her eyes were as soft as Mistress Anne's, and nearly of the same exquisite brown, which made the damsel blush and experience a revival of the old feeling of her childhood, as if he put her under a spell.

He went on to say that he had had the good fortune to pick up and restore to Queen Mary Beatrice a gold and coral rosary which she had dropped on her way to St. James's Palace from Whitehall. She thanked him graciously, letting him kiss her hand, and asking him if he were of the true Church. 'Imagine my father's feelings,' he added, 'when she said, "Ah! but you will be ere long; I give it you as a pledge."'

He produced the rosary, handing it first to Anne, who admired the beautiful filigree work, but it was almost snatched from her by Mrs. Archfield, who wound it twice on her tiny wrist, tried to get it over her head, and did everything but ask for it, till her husband, turning round, said roughly, 'Give it back, madam. We want no Popish toys here.'

Lucy put in a hasty question whether Master Oakshott had seen much sport, and this led to a spirited description of the homely earnest of wild boar hunting under the great Elector of Brandenburg, in contrast with the splendours of *la chasse aux sangliers* at Fontainebleau with the green and gold uniforms, the fanfares on the curled horns, the ladies in their coaches, forced to attend whether ill or well, the very boars themselves too well bred not to conform to the sport of the great idol of France. And again, he showed the diamond sleeve buttons, the trophies of a sort of bazaar held at Marly, where the stalls were kept by the Dauphin, Monsieur, the Duke of Maine, Madame de Maintenon, and the rest, where the purchases were winnings at Ombre, made not with coin but with nominal sums, and other games at cards, and all was given away that was not purchased. And again the levees, when the King's wig was handed through the curtains on a stick. Peregrine's profane mimicry of the stately march of Louis Quatorze, and the cringing obeisances of his courtiers, together with their strutting majesty towards their own inferiors, convulsed all with merriment; and the bride shrieked out, 'Do it again! Oh, I shall die of laughing!'

It was very girlish, with a silvery ring, but the elder ladies looked round, and the bridegroom muttered 'Mountebank.'

The fiddler arrived at that moment, and the young people paired off, the young couple naturally together, and Peregrine, to the surprise and perhaps discomfiture of more than one visitor, securing Anne's hand. The young lady pupils of Madame knew their steps, and Lucy danced correctly, Anne with an easy, stately grace, Charles Archfield performed his *devoir* seriously, his little wife frisked with childish glee, evidently quite untaught, but Peregrine's light narrow feet sprang, pointed themselves, and bounded with trained agility, set off by the tight blackness of his suit. He was like one of the grotesque figures shaped in black paper, or as Sir Philip, looking in from the dining-parlour, observed, 'like a light-heeled French fop.'

As a rule partners retained one another all the evening, but little Mrs. Archfield knew no etiquette, and maybe her husband had pushed and pulled her into place a little more authoritatively than she quite approved, for she shook him off, and turning round to Peregrine exclaimed—

'Now, I will dance with you! You do leap and hop so high and trippingly! Never mind her; she is only a parson's niece!'

'Madam!' exclaimed Charles, in a tone of surprised displeasure; but she only nodded archly at him, and said, 'I must dance with him; he can jump so high.'

'Let her have her way,' whispered Lucy, 'she is but a child, and it will be better not to make a pother.'

He yielded, though with visible annoyance, asking Anne if she would put up with a poor deserted swain, and as he led her off muttering, 'That fellow's friskiness is like to be taken out of him at Oakwood.'

Meanwhile the small creature had taken possession of her chosen partner, who, so far as size went, was far better suited to her than any of the other men present. They were dancing something original and unpremeditated, with twirls and springs, sweeps and bends, bounds and footings, just as the little lady's fancy prompted, perhaps guided in some degree by her partner's experience of national dances. White and black, they figured about, she with floating sheeny hair and glistening robes, he trim and tight and jetty, like fairy and imp! It was so droll and pretty that talkers and dancers alike paused to watch them in a strange fascination, till at last, quite breathless and pink as a moss rosebud, Alice dropped upon a chair near her husband. He stood grim, stiff, and vexed, all the more because Peregrine had taken her fan and was using it so as to make it wave like butterfly's wings, while poor Charles looked, as the Doctor whispered to his father, far more inclined to lay it about her ears.

Sir Philip laughed heartily, for both he and the Doctor had been so much entranced and amused as to be far more diverted at the lad's discomfiture than scandalised at the bride's escapade, which they viewed as child's play.'

Perhaps, however, he was somewhat comforted by her later observation, 'He is as ugly as Old Nick, and looks like always laughing at you; but I wish you could dance like him, Mr. Archfield, only then you wouldn't be my dear old great big husband, or so beautiful to look at. Oh yes, to be sure, he is nothing but a skipjack such as one makes out of a chicken bone!'

And Anne meanwhile was exclaiming to her mother, 'Oh, madam! how could they do such a thing? How could they make poor Charley marry that foolish ill-mannered little creature?'

'Hush, daughter, you must drop that childish name,' said Mrs. Woodford gravely.

Anne blushed. 'I forgot, madam, but I am so sorry for him.'

'There is no reason for uneasiness, my dear. She is a mere child, and under such hands as Lady Archfield she is sure to improve. It is far better that she should be so young, as it will be the more easy to mould her.'

'I hope there is any stuff in her to be moulded,' sighed the maiden.

'My dear child,' returned her mother, 'I cannot permit you to talk in this manner. Yes, I know Mr. Archfield has been as a brother to you, but even his sister ought not to allow herself to discuss or dwell on what she deems the shortcomings of his wife.'

The mother in her prudence had silenced the girl; but none the less did each fall asleep with a sad and foreboding heart. She knew her child to be good and well-principled, but those early days of notice and petting from the young Princesses of the House of York had never faded from the childish mind, and although Anne was dutiful, cheerful, and outwardly contented, the mother often suspected that over the spinning-wheel or embroidery frame she indulged in day dreams of heroism, promotion, and grandeur, which might either fade away in a happy life of domestic duty or become temptations.

Before going away next morning Peregrine entreated that Mistress Anne might have the Queen's rosary, but her mother decidedly refused. 'It ought to be an heirloom in your family,' said she.

He threw up his hands with one of his strange gestures.

CHAPTER IX

ON HIS TRAVELS

'For Satan finds some mischief still
For idle hands to do.'
ISAAC WATTS.

PEREGRINE went off in good spirits, promising a visit on his return to London, of which he seemed to have no doubt; but no more was heard of him for ten days. At the end of that time the Portsmouth carrier conveyed the following note to Winchester:—

HONOURED AND REVEREND SIR—Seven years since your arguments and intercession induced my father to consent to what I hoped had been the rescue of me, body and soul. I know not whether to ask of your goodness to make the same endeavour again. My father declares that nothing shall induce him again to let me go abroad with my uncle, and persists in declaring that the compact has been broken by our visits to Papist lands, nor will aught that I can say persuade him that the Muscovite abhors the Pope quite as much as he can. He likewise deems that having unfortunately become his heir, I must needs remain at home to thin the timber and watch the ploughmen; and when I have besought him to let me yield my place to Robert he replies that I am playing the part of Esau. I have written to my uncle, who has been a true father to me, and would be loth to part from me for his own sake as well as mine, but I know not whether he will be able to prevail; and I entreat of you, reverend sir, to add your persuasions, for I well know that it would be my perdition to remain bound where I am.

Commend me to Mrs. Woodford and Mistress Anne. I trust that the former is in better health.—I remain, reverend sir, Your humble servant to command,

PEREGRINE OAKSHOTT.

Given at Oakwood House,
 This 10*th of October* 1687.

This was very bad news, but Dr. Woodford knew not how to interfere; moreover, being in course at the Cathedral, he could not absent himself long enough for an expedition to Oakwood, through wintry roads in short days. He could only write an encouraging letter to the poor lad, and likewise one to Mr. Horncastle, who under the Indulgence had a chapel of his own. The Doctor had kept up the acquaintance formed by Peregrine's accident, and had come to regard him with much esteem, and as likely to exercise a wholesome influence upon his patron. Nothing more was heard for a week, and then came another visitor to the Doctor's door, Sir Peregrine himself, on his way down, at considerable inconvenience, to endeavour to prevail with his brother to allow him to retain his nephew in his suite.

'Surely,' he said, 'my brother had enough of camps in his youth to understand that his son will be none the worse squire for having gone a little beyond Hampshire bogs, and learnt what the world is made of.'

'I cannot tell,' said Dr. Woodford; 'I have my fears that he thinks the less known of the world the better.'

'That might answer with a heavy clod of a lad such as the poor youth who is gone, and such as, for his own sake and my brother's, I trust the younger one is, *fruges consumere natus;* but as for this boy, dulness and vacancy are precisely what would be the ruin of him. Let my brother keep Master Robert at home, and give him Oakwood; I will provide for Perry as I always promised to do.'

'If he is wise he will accept the offer,' said

Dr. Woodford; 'but 'tis hard to be wise for others.'

'Nothing harder, sir. I would that I had gone home with Perry, but mine audience of his Majesty was fixed for the ensuing week, and my brother's summons was peremptory.'

'I trust your honour will prevail,' said Mrs. Woodford gently. 'You have effected a mighty change in the poor boy, and I can well believe that he is as a son to you.'

'Well, madam, yes—as sons go,' said the knight in a somewhat disappointing tone.

She looked at him anxiously, and ventured to murmur a hope so very like an inquiry, and so full of solicitous hope, that it actually unlocked the envoy's reserve, and he said, 'Ah, madam, you have been the best mother that the poor youth has ever had! I will speak freely to you, for should I fail in overcoming my brother's prejudices, you will be able to do more for him than any one else, and I know you will be absolutely secret.'

Mrs. Woodford sighed, with forebodings of not long being able to aid any one in this world, but still she listened with earnest interest and sympathy.

'Yes, madam, you implanted in him that which yet may conquer his strange nature. Your name is as it were a charm to conjure up his better spirit.'

'Of course,' she said, 'I never durst hope, that he could be tamed and under control all at once, but——' and she paused.

'He has improved—vastly improved,' said the uncle. 'Indeed, when first I took him with me, while he was still weak, and moreover much overcome by sea-sickness, while all was strange to him, and he was relieved by not finding himself treated as an outcast, I verily thought him meeker than other urchins, and that the outcry against him was unmerited. But no sooner had we got to Berlin, and while I was as yet too busy to provide either masters or occupations for my young gentleman, than he did indeed make me feel that I had charge of a young imp, and that if I did not watch the better, it might be a case of war with his Spanish Majesty. For would you believe it, his envoy's gardens joined ours, and what must my young master do, but sit atop of our wall, making grimaces at the dons and donnas as they paced the walks, and pelting them from time to time with walnuts. Well, I was mindful of your counsel, and did not flog him, nor let my chaplain do so, though I know the good man's fingers itched to be at him; but I reasoned with him on the harm he was doing me, and would you believe it, the poor lad burst into tears, and implored me to give him something to do, to save him from his own spirit. I set him to write out and translate a long roll of Latin despatches sent up by that pedant Court in Hungary, and I declare to you I had no more trouble with him till next he was left idle. I gave him tutors, and he studied with fervour, and made progress at which they were amazed. He learnt the High Dutch faster than any other of my people, and could soon jabber away in it with the best of the Elector's folk, and I began to think I had a nephew who would do me no small credit. I sent him to perfect his studies at Leyden, but shall I confess it to you? it was to find that no master nor discipline could keep him out of the riotings and quarrels of the worse sort of students. Nay, I found him laid by with a rapier thrust

in the side from a duel, for no better cause
than biting his thumb at a Scots law student
in chapel, his apology being that to sit
through a Dutch sermon drove him crazy.
'Tis not that he is not trustworthy. Find
employment for the restless demon that is in
him, and all is well with him; moreover, he
is full of wit and humour, and beguiles a long
journey or tedious evening at an inn better
than any comrade I ever knew, extracting
mirth from all around, even the very discomforts, and searching to the quick all that is to
be seen. But if left to himself, the restless
demon that preys on him is sure to set him
to something incalculable. At Turin it set
him to scraping acquaintance with a Capuchin
friar, a dirty rogue whom I would have kept
on the opposite side of the street. That was
his graver mood; but what more must he do,
but borrow or steal, I know not how, the
ghastly robes of the Confraternity of Death
—the white garb and peaked cap with two
holes for the eyes, wherewith men of all
degrees disguise themselves while doing the
pious work of bearing the dead to the grave.
None suspected him, for the disguise is com-

plete, and a duke may walk unknown beside a water-carrier, bearing the corpse of a cobbler. All would have been well, but that at the very brink of the grave the boy's fiend —'tis his own word—impelled him to break forth into his wild " Ho! ho! ho!" with an eldritch shriek, and slipping out of his cerements, dash off headlong over the wall of the cemetery. He was not followed. I believe the poor body belonged to a fellow whose salvation was more than doubtful in spite of all the priests could do, and that the bearers really took him for the foul fiend. It was not till a week or two after that the ring of his voice and laugh caused him to be recognised by one of the Duke of Savoy's gentlemen, happily a prudent man, loth to cause a tumult against one of my suite, and he told me all privately in warning. Ay, and when I spoke to Peregrine, I found him thoroughly penitent at having insulted the dead; he had been unhappy ever since, and had actually bestowed his last pocket-piece on the widow. He made handsome apologies in good Italian, which he had picked up as fast as the German, to the gentleman, who promised that it should

go no farther, and kept his word. It was
the solemnity, Peregrine assured me, that
brought back all the intolerableness of the
preachings at home, and awoke the same
demon.'

'How long ago was this, sir?'

'About eighteen months.'

'And has all been well since?'

· 'Fairly well. He has had fuller and more
responsible work to do for me, his turn for
languages making him a most valuable secretary ; and in the French Court, really the
most perilous of all to a young man's virtue,
he behaved himself well. It is not debauchery
that he has a taste for, but he must be doing
something, and if wholesome occupations do
not stay his appetite, he will be doing mischief. He brought on himself a very serious
rebuke from the Prince of Orange, churlishly
and roughly given, I allow, but fully merited,
for making grimaces at his acquaintance
among the young officers at a military inspection. Heaven help the lad if he be left
with his father, whose most lively notion of
innocent sport is scratching the heads of his
hogs!'

Nothing could be said in answer save earnest wishes that the knight might persuade his brother. Mrs. Woodford wished her brother-in-law to go with him to add force to his remonstrance; but on the whole it was thought better to leave the family to themselves, Dr. Woodford only writing to Major Oakshott, as well as to the youth himself.

The result was anxiously watched for, and in another week, earlier in the day than Mrs. Woodford was able to leave her room, Sir Peregrine's horses stopped at the door, and as Anne ascertained by a peep from the window, he was only accompanied by his servants.

'Yes,' he said to the Doctor in his vexation, 'one would really think that by force of eating Southdown mutton my poor brother had acquired the brains of one of his own rams! I declare 'tis a piteous sight to see a man resolute on ruining his son and breaking his own heart all for conscience sake!'

'Say you so, sir! I had hoped that the sight of what you have made of your nephew might have had some effect.'

'All the effect it has produced is to make

him more determined to take him from me. The Hampshire mind abhors foreign breeding, and the old Cromwellian spirit thinks good manners sprung from the world, and wit from the Evil One!'

'I can quite believe that Peregrine's courtly airs are not welcomed here; I could see what our good neighbour, Sir Philip Archfield, thought of them; but whereas no power on earth could make the young gentleman a steady-going clownish youth after his father's heart, methought he might prefer his present polish to impishness.'

'So I told him, but I might as well have talked to the horse block. It is his duty, quotha, to breed his heir up in godly simplicity!'

'Simplicity is all very well to begin with, but once flown, it cannot be restored.'

'And that is what my brother cannot see. Well, my poor boy must be left to his fate. There is no help for it, and all I can hope is that you, sir, and the ladies, will stand his friend, and do what may lie in your power to make him patient and render his life less intolerable.'

'Indeed, sir, we will do what we can; I wish that I could hope that it would be of much service.'

'My brother has more respect for your advice than perhaps you suppose; and to you, madam, the poor lad looks with earnest gratitude. Nay, even his mother reaps the benefit of the respect with which you have inspired him. Peregrine treats her with a gentleness and attention such as she never knew before from her bear cubs. Poor soul! I think she likes it, though it somewhat perplexes her, and she thinks it all French manners. There is one more favour, your reverence, which I scarce dare lay before you. You have seen my black boy Hans?'

'He was with you at Oakwood seven years ago.'

'Even so. I bought the poor fellow when a mere child from a Dutch skipper who had used him scurvily, and he has grown up as faithful as a very spaniel, and mightily useful too, not only as body servant, but he can cook as well as any French *maître d'hôtel*, froth chocolate, and make the best coffee I ever tasted; is as honest as the day, and, I believe, would lay down his life for Peregrine or me. I shall be cruelly at a loss without him, but a physician I met in London tells me it would be no better than murder to take the poor rogue to so cold a country as Muscovy. I would leave him to wait on Perry, but they will not hear of it at Oakwood. My sister-in-law wellnigh had a fit every time she looked at him when I was there before, and I found, moreover, that even when I was at hand, the servants jeered at the poor blackamoor, gave him his meals apart, and only the refuse of their own, so that he would fare but ill if I left him to their mercy. I had thought of offering him to Mr. Evelyn of Says Court, who would no doubt use him well, but it was Peregrine who suggested that if you of your goodness would receive the poor fellow, they could sometimes meet, and that would cheer his heart, and he really is far from a useless knave, but is worth two of any serving-men I ever saw.'

To take an additional man-servant was by no means such a great proposal as it would be in most houses at present. Men swarmed in much larger proportion than maids in all families of condition, and the Doctor was wealthy enough for one—more or less—to make little difference, but the question was asked as to what wages Hans should receive.

The knight laughed. 'Wages, poor lad, what should he do with them? He is but a slave, I tell you. Meat, clothes, and fire, that is all he needs, and I will so deal with him that he will serve you in all faithfulness and obedience. He can speak English enough to know what you bid him do, but not enough for chatter with the servants.'

So the agreement was made, and poor Hans was to be sent down by the Portsmouth coach together with Peregrine's luggage.

CHAPTER X

THE MENAGERIE

> ' The head remains unchanged within,
>   Nor altered much the face,
> It still retains its native grin,
>   And all its old grimace.
>
> ' Men with contempt the brute surveyed,
>   Nor would a name bestow,
> But women liked the motley beast,
>   And called the thing a beau.'
>   *The Monkies*, MERRICK.

THE Woodford family did not long remain at Winchester. Anne declared the cold to be harming her mother, and became very anxious to bring her to the milder sea breezes of Portchester, and though Mrs. Woodford had little expectation that any place would make much difference to her, she was willing to return to the quiet and repose of her home under the castle walls beside the tranquil sea.

Thus they travelled back, as soon as the Doctor's Residence was ended, plodding through the heavy chalk roads as well as the big horses could drag the cumbrous coach up and down the hills, only halting for much needed rest at Sir Philip Archfield's red house, round three sides of a quadrangle, the fourth with a low wall backed by a row of poplar-trees, looking out on the alternate mud and sluggish waters of Fareham creek, but with a beautiful garden behind the house.

The welcome was hearty. Lady Archfield at once conducted Mrs. Woodford to her own bedroom, where she was to rest and be served apart, and Anne disrobed her of her wraps, covered her upon the bed, and at her hostess's desire was explaining what refreshment would best suit her, when there was a shrill voice at the door: 'I want Mistress Anne! I want to show her my clothes and jewels.'

'Coming, child, she is coming when she has attended to her mother,' responded the lady. 'White wine, or red, did you say, Anne, and a little ginger?'

'Is she never coming?' was again the

call; and Lady Archfield muttering, 'Was there ever such an impatient poppet?' released Anne, who was instantly pounced upon by young Mrs. Archfield. Linking her arm into that of her visitor, and thrusting Lucy into the background, the little heiress proceeded to her own wainscotted bedroom, bare according to modern views, but very luxurious according to those of the seventeenth century, and with the toilet apparatus, scanty indeed, but of solid silver, and with a lavish amount of perfumery. Her 'own woman' was in waiting to display and refold the whole wedding wardrobe, brocade, satin, taffetas, cambric, Valenciennes, and point d'Alençon. Anne had to admire each in detail, and then to give full meed to the whole casket of jewels, numerous and dazzling as befitted a constellation of heirlooms upon one small head. They were beautiful, but it was wearisome to repeat 'Vastly pretty!' 'How exquisite!' 'That becomes you very well,' almost mechanically, when Lucy was standing about all the time, longing to exchange the girlish confidences that were burning to come forth. 'Young Madam,' as every one called her in those times when Christian names were at a discount, seemed to be jealous of attention to any one else, and the instant she saw the guest attempt to converse with her sister-in-law peremptorily interrupted, almost as if affronted.

Perhaps if Anne had enjoyed freedom of speech with Lucy she would not have learnt as much as did her mother, for the young are often more scrupulous as to confidences than their seniors, who view them as still children, and freely discuss their affairs among themselves.

So Lady Archfield poured out her troubles: how her daughter-in-law refused employment, and disdained instruction in needlework, housewifery, or any domestic art, how she jangled the spinnet, but would not learn music, and was unoccupied, fretful, and exacting, a burthen to herself and every one else, and treating Lucy as the slave of her whims and humours. As to such discipline as mothers-in-law were wont to exercise upon young wives, the least restraint or contradiction provoked such a tempest of passion as to shake the tiny, delicate frame to a degree that alarmed the good old matron for the consequences. Her health was a continual difficulty, for her constitution was very frail, every imprudence cost her suffering, and yet any check to her impulses as to food, exertion, or encountering weather was met by a spoilt child's resentment. Moreover, her young husband, and even his father, always thought the ladies were hard upon her, and would not have her vexed; and as their presence always brightened and restrained her, they never understood the full amount of her petulance and waywardness, and when they found her out of spirits, or out of temper, they charged all on her ailments or on want of consideration from her mother and sister-in-law.

Poor Lady Archfield, it was trying for her that her husband should be nearly as blind as his son. The young husband was wonderfully tender, indulgent, and patient with the little creature, but it would not be easy to say whether the affection were not a good deal like that for his dog or his horse, as something absolutely his own, with which no one else had a right to interfere. It was a relief to the family that she always wanted to be out of doors with him whenever the weather permitted, nay, often when it was far from suitable to so fragile a being ; but if she came home aching and crying ever so much with chill or fatigue, even if she had to keep her bed afterwards, she was equally determined to rush out as soon as she was up again, and as angry as ever at remonstrance.

Charles was gone to try a horse ; and as the remains of the effects of her last imprudence had prevented her accompanying him, the arrival of the guests had been a welcome diversion to the monotony of the morning.

He was, however, at home again by the time the dinner-bell summoned the younger ladies from the inspection of the trinkets and the gentlemen from the live stock, all to sit round the heavy oaken table draped with the whitest of napery, spun by Lady Archfield in her maiden days, and loaded with substantial joints, succeeded by delicacies manufactured by herself and Lucy.

As to the horse, Charles was fairly satisfied, but 'that fellow, young Oakshott, had been after him, and had the refusal.'

'Don't you be outbid, Mr. Archfield,'

exclaimed the wife. 'What is the matter of a few guineas to us?'

'Little fear,' replied Charles. 'The old Major is scarcely like to pay down twenty gold caroluses, but if he should, the bay is his.'

'Oh, but why not offer thirty?' she cried.

Charles laughed. 'That would be a scurvy trick, sweetheart, and if Peregrine be a crooked stick, we need not be crooked too.'

'I was about to ask,' said the Doctor, 'whether you had heard aught of that same young gentleman.'

'I have seen him where I never desire to see him again,' said Sir Philip, 'riding as though he would be the death of the poor hounds.'

'Nick Huntsman swears that he bewitches them,' said Charles, 'for they always lose the scent when he is in the field, but I believe 'tis the wry looks of him that throw them all out.'

'And I say,' cried the inconsistent bride, 'that 'tis all jealousy that puts the gentlemen beside themselves, because none of them can dance, nor make a bow, nor hand a cup of chocolate, nor open a gate on horseback like him.'

'What does a man on horseback want with opening gates?' exclaimed Charles.

'That's your manners, sir,' said young madam with a laugh. 'What's the poor lady to do while her cavalier flies over and leaves her in the lurch?'

Her husband did not like the general laugh, and muttered, 'You know what I mean well enough.'

'Yes, so do I! To fumble at the fastening till your poor beast can bear it no longer and swerves aside, and I sit waiting a good half hour before you bring down your pride enough to alight and open it.'

'All because you *would* send Will home for your mask.'

'You would like to have had my poor little face one blister with the glare of sun and sea.'

'Blisters don't come at this time of the year.'

'No, nor to those who have no complexion to lose,' she cried, with a triumphant look at the two maidens, who certainly had not the lilies nor the roses that she believed herself to have, though, in truth, her imprudences had left her paler and less pretty than at Winchester.

If this were the style of the matrimonial conversations, Anne again grieved for her old playfellow, and she perceived that Lucy looked uncomfortable; but there was no getting a moment's private conversation with her before the coach was brought round again for the completion of the journey. All that neighbourhood had a very bad reputation as the haunt of lawless characters, prone to violence; and though among mere smugglers there was little danger of an attack on persons well known like the Woodford family, they were often joined by far more desperate men from the seaport, so that it was never desirable to be out of doors after dark.

The journey proved to have been too much for Mrs. Woodford's strength, and for some days she was so ill that Anne never left the house; but she rallied again, and on coming downstairs became very anxious that her daughter should not be more confined by attendance than was wholesome, and insisted on every opportunity of change or amusement being taken.

One day as Anne was in the garden she was surprised by Peregrine dashing up on horseback.

'You would not take the Queen's rosary before,' he said. 'You must now, to save it. My father has smelt it out. He says it is teraphim! Micah—Rachel, what not, are quoted against it. He would have smashed it into fragments, but that Martha Browning said it would be a pretty bracelet. I'd sooner see it smashed than on her red fist. To think of her giving in to such vanities! But he said she might have it, only to be new strung. When he was gone, she said, "I don't really want the thing, but it was hard you should lose the Queen's keepsake. Can you bestow it safely?" I said I could, and brought it hither. Keep it, Anne, I pray.'

Anne hesitated, and referred it to her mother upstairs.

'Tell him,' she said, 'that we will keep it in trust for him as a royal gift.'

Peregrine was disappointed, but had to be content.

A Dutch vessel from the East Indies had brought home sundry strange animals, which were exhibited at the Jolly Mariner at Portsmouth, and thus announced on a bill printed on execrable paper, brought out to Portchester by some of the market people :—

'An Ellefante twice the Bignesse of an Ocks, the Trunke or Probosces whereof can pick up a Needle or roote up an Ellum Tree. Also the Royale Tyger, the same as has slaine and devoured seven yonge Gentoo babes, three men, and two women at the township at Chuttergong, nie to Bombay, in the Eastern Indies. Also the sacred Ape, worshipped by the heathen of the Indies, the Dancing Serpent which weareth Spectacles, and whose Bite is instantly mortal, with other rare Fish, Fowle, Idols and the like. All to be seene at the Charge of one Groat per head.'

Mrs. Woodford declared herself to be extremely desirous that her daughter should see and bring home an account of all these marvels, and though Anne had no great inclination to face the tiger with the formidable appetite, she could not refuse to accompany her uncle.

The Jolly Mariner stood in one of the foulest and narrowest of the streets of the unsavoury seaport, and Dr. Woodford sighed, and fumed, and wished for a good pipe of tobacco more than once as he hesitated to try to force a way for his niece through the throng round the entrance to the stable-yard of the Jolly Mariner, apparently too rough to pay respect to gown and cassock. Anne clung to his arm, ready to give up the struggle, but a voice said, 'Allow me, sir. Mistress Anne, deign to take my arm.'

It was Peregrine Oakshott with his brother Robert, and she could hardly tell how in a few seconds she had been squeezed through the crowd, and stood in the inn-yard, in a comparatively free space, for a groat was a prohibitory charge to the vulgar.

'Peregrine! Master Oakshott!' They heard an exclamation of pleasure, at which Peregrine shrugged his shoulders and looked expressively at Anne, before turning to receive the salutations of an elderly gentleman and a tall young woman, very plainly but handsomely clad in mourning deeper than his own. She was of a tall, gaunt, angular figure, and a face that never could have been handsome, and now bore evident traces of smallpox in redness and pits.

Dr. Woodford knew the guardian Mr. Browning, and his ward Mistress Martha and Mistress Anne Jacobina were presented to one another. The former gave a good-humoured smile, as if perfectly unconscious of her own want of beauty, and declared she had hoped to meet all the rest here, especially Mistress Anne Woodford, of whom she had heard so much. There was just a little patronage about the tone which repelled the proud spirit that was in Anne, and in spite of the ordinary dread and repulsion she felt for Peregrine, she was naughty enough to have the feeling of a successful beauty when Peregrine most manifestly turned away from the heiress in her silk and velvet to do the honours of the exhibition to the parson's niece.

The elephant was fastened by the leg to a post, which perhaps he could have pulled up, had he thought it worth his while, but he was well contented to wave his trunk about and extend its clever finger to receive contributions of cakes and apples, and he was too well amused to resort to any strong measures. The tiger, to Anne's relief, proved to be only a stuffed specimen. Peregrine, who had seen a good many foreign animals in Holland, where the Dutch captains were in the habit of bringing curiosities home for the delectation of their families in their *Lusthausen*, was a very amusing companion, having much to tell about bird and beast, while Robert stood staring with open mouth. The long-legged secretary and the beautiful doves were, however, only stuffed, but Anne was much entertained at second hand with the relation of the numerous objects, which on the word of a Leyden merchant had been known to disappear in the former bird's capacious crop, and with stories of the graceful dancing of the cobra, though she was not sorry that the present specimen was only visible in a bottle of arrack, where his spectacled hood was scarcely apparent. Presently a well-known shrill young voice was heard. 'Yes, yes, I

know I shall swoon at that terrible tiger!
Oh, don't! I can't come any farther.'

'Why, you would come, madam,' said
Charles.

'Yes, yes! but—oh, there's a two-tailed
monster! I know it is the tiger! It is
moving! I shall die if you take me any
farther.'

'Plague upon your folly, madam! It is
only the elephant,' said a gruffer, rude voice.

'Oh, it is dreadful! 'Tis like a mountain!
I can't! Oh no, I can't!'

'Come, madam, you have brought us thus
far, you must come on, and not make fools of
us all,' said Charles's voice. 'There's nothing
to hurt you.'

Anne, understanding the distress and per-
plexity, here turned back to the passage into
the court, and began persuasively to explain
to little Mrs. Archfield that the tiger was
dead, and only a skin, and that the elephant
was the mildest of beasts, till she coaxed
forward that small personage, who had of
course never really intended to turn back,
supported and guarded as she was by her
husband, and likewise by a tall, glittering

figure in big boots and a handsome scarlet uniform and white feather who claimed her attention as he strode into the court. 'Ha! Mistress Anne and the Doctor on my life. What, don't you know me?'

'Master Sedley Archfield!' said the Doctor; 'welcome home, sir! 'Tis a meeting of old acquaintance. You and this gentleman are both so much altered that it is no wonder if you do not recognise one another at once.'

'No fear of Mr. Perry Oakshott not being recognised,' said Sedley Archfield, holding out his hand, but with a certain sneer in his rough voice that brought Peregrine's eyebrows together. 'Kenspeckle enough, as the fools of Whigs say in Scotland.'

'Are you long from Scotland, sir?' asked Dr. Woodford, by way of preventing personalities.

'Oh ay, sir; these six months and more. There's not much more sport to be had since the fools of Cameronians have been pretty well got under, and 'tis no loss to be at Hounslow.'

'And oh, what a fright!' exclaimed Mrs.

Archfield, catching sight of the heiress. 'Keep her away! She makes me ill.'

They were glad to divert her attention to feeding the elephant, and she was coquetting a little about making up her mind to approach even the defunct tiger, while she insisted on having the number of his victims counted over to her. Anne asked for Lucy, to whom she wanted to show the pigeons, but was answered that, 'My lady wanted Lucy at home over some matter of jellies and blancmanges.'

Charles shrugged his shoulders a little and Sedley grumbled to Anne, 'The little vixen sets her heart on cates that she won't lay a finger to make, and poor Lucy is like to be no better than a cook-maid, while they won't cross her, for fear of her tantrums.'

At that instant piercing screams, shriek upon shriek, rang through the court, and turning hastily round, Anne beheld a little monkey perched on Mrs. Archfield's head, having apparently leapt thither from the pole to which it was chained.

The keeper was not in sight, being in fact employed over a sale of some commodities within. There was a general springing to the rescue. Charles tried to take the creature off, Sedley tugged at the chain fastened to a belt round its body, but the monkey held tight by the curls on the lady's forehead with its hands, and crossed its legs round her neck, clasping the hands so that the effect of the attempts of her husband and his cousin was only to throttle her, so that she could no longer scream and was almost in a fit, when on Peregrine holding out a nut and speaking coaxingly in Dutch, the monkey unloosed its hold, and with another bound was on his arm. He stood caressing and feeding it, talking to it in the same tongue, while it made little squeaks and chatterings, evidently delighted, though its mournful old man's visage still had the same piteous expression. There was something most grotesque and almost weird in the sight of Peregrine's queer figure toying with its odd hands which seemed to be in black gloves, and the strange language he talked to it added to the uncanny effect. Even the Doctor felt it as he stood watching, and would have muttered 'Birds of a feather,' but that the words were spoken more gruffly and plainly by Sedley Archfield, who said something about the Devil and his dam, which the good Doctor did not choose to hear, and only said to Peregrine, 'You know how to deal with the jackanapes.'

'I have seen some at Leyden, sir. This is a pretty little beast.'

Pretty! There was a recoil in horror, for the creature looked to the crowd demoniacal. Something the same was the sensation of Charles, who, assisted by Anne and Martha, had been rather carrying than leading his wife into the inn parlour, where she immediately had a fit of hysterics—vapours, as they called it—bringing all the women of the inn about her, while Martha and Anne soothed her as best they could, and he was reduced to helplessly leaning out at the bay window.

When the sobs and cries subsided, under cold water and essences without and strong waters within, and the little lady in Martha's strong arms, between the matronly coaxing of the fat hostess and the kind soothings of the two young ladies, had been restored to something of equanimity, Mistress Martha laid her down and said with the utmost good humour and placidity to the young husband, ' Now I'll go, sir. She is better now, but the sight of my face might set her off again.'

'Oh, do not say so, madam. We are infinitely obliged. Let her thank you.'

But Martha shook her hand and laughed, turning to leave the room, so that he was fain to give her his arm and escort her back to her guardian.

Then ensued a scream. 'Where's he going? Mr. Archfield, don't leave me.'

'He is only taking Mistress Browning back to her guardian,' said Anne.

'Eh? oh, how can he? A hideous fright!' she cried.

To say the truth, she was rather pleased to have had such a dreadful adventure, and to have made such a commotion, though she protested that she must go home directly, and could never bear the sight of those dreadful monsters again, or she should die on the spot.

' But,' said she, when the coach was at the door, and Anne had restored her dress to its dainty gaiety, ' I must thank Master Peregrine for taking off that horrible jackanapes.'

'Small thanks to him,' said Charles crossly. 'I wager it was all his doing out of mere spite.'

'He is too good a beau ever to spite *me*,' said Mrs. Alice, her head a little on one side.

'Then to show off what he could do with the beast—Satan's imp, like himself.'

'No, no, Mr. Archfield,' pleaded Anne, 'that was impossible; I saw him myself. He was with that sailor-looking man measuring the height of the secretary bird.'

'I believe you are always looking after him,' grumbled Charles. 'I can't guess what all the women see in him to be always gazing after him.'

'Because he is so charmingly ugly,' laughed the young wife, tripping out in utter forgetfulness that she was to die if she went near the beasts again. She met Peregrine halfway across the yard with outstretched hands, exclaiming—

'O Mr. Oakshott! it was so good in you to take away that nasty beast.'

'I am glad, madam, to have been of use,' said Peregrine, bowing and smiling, a smile that might explain something of his fascination. 'The poor brute was only drawn, as all of our kind are. He wanted to see so sweet a lady nearer. He is quite harmless. Will you stroke him? See, there he sits, gazing after you. Will you give him a cake and make friends?'

'No, no, madam, it cannot be; it is too much,' grumbled Charles; and though Alice had backed at first, perhaps for the pleasure of teasing him, or for that of being the centre of observation, actually, with all manner of pretty airs and graces, she let herself be led forward, lay a timid hand on the monkey's head, and put a cake in its black fingers, while all the time Peregrine held it fast and talked Dutch to it; and Charles Archfield hardly contained his rage, though Anne endeavoured to argue the impossibility of Peregrine's having incited the attack; and Sedley blustered that they ought to interfere and make the fellow know the reason why. However, Charles had sense enough to know that though he might exhale his vexation in grumbling, he had no valid cause for quarrelling with young Oakshott, so he contented himself with black looks and grudging thanks, as he was obliged to let Peregrine hand his wife into her carriage amid her nods and becks and wreathed smiles.

They would have taken Dr. Woodford and his niece home in the coach, but Anne had an errand in the town, and preferred to return by boat. She wanted some oranges and Turkey figs to allay her mother's constant thirst, and Peregrine begged permission to accompany them, saying that he knew where to find the best and cheapest. Accordingly he took them to a tiny cellar, in an alley by the boat camber, where the Portugal oranges certainly looked riper and were cheaper than any that Anne had found before; but there seemed to be an odd sort of understanding between Peregrine and the withered old weatherbeaten sailor who sold them, such as rather puzzled the Doctor.

'I hope these are not contraband,' he said to Peregrine, when the oranges had been packed in the basket of the servant who followed them.

Peregrine shrugged his shoulders.

'Living is hard, sir. Ask no questions.'

The Doctor looked tempted to turn back

with the fruit, but such doubts were viewed as ultra scruples, and would hardly have been entertained even by a magistrate such as Sir Philip Archfield.

It was not a time for questions, and Peregrine remained with them till they embarked at the point, asking to be commended to Mrs. Woodford, and hoping soon to come and see both her and poor Hans, he left them.

CHAPTER XI

PROPOSALS

Hear me, ye venerable core,
  As counsel for poor mortals,
That frequent pass douce Wisdom's door
  For glaikit Folly's portals;
I for their thoughtless, careless sakes
  Would here propose defences,
Their doucie tricks, their black mistakes,
  Their failings and mischances.'
                      BURNS.

FOR seven years Anne Woodford had kept Lucy Archfield's birthday with her, and there was no refusing now, though there was more and more unwillingness to leave Mrs. Woodford, whose declining state became so increasingly apparent that even the loving daughter could no longer be blind to it.

The coach was sent over to fetch Mistress Anne to Fareham, and the invalid was left, comfortably installed in her easy-chair by the parlour fire, with a little table by her side, holding a hand-bell, a divided orange, a glass of toast and water, and the Bible and Prayerbook, wherein lay her chief studies, together with a little needlework, which still amused her feeble hands. The Doctor, divided between his parish, his study, and his garden, had promised to look in from time to time.

Presently, however, the door was gently tapped, and on her call 'Come in,' Hans, all one grin, admitted Peregrine Oakshott, bowing low in his foreign, courteous manner, and entreating her to excuse his intrusion, 'For truly, madam, in your goodness is my only hope.'

Then he knelt on one knee and kissed the hand she held out to him, while desiring him to speak freely to her.

'Nay, madam, I fear I shall startle you, when I lay before you the only chance that can aid me to overcome the demon that is in me.'

'My poor——'

'Call me your boy, as when I was here seven years ago. Let me sit at your feet as then and listen to me.'

'Indeed I will, my dear boy,' and she laid her hand on his dark head. 'Tell me all that is in your heart.'

'Ah, dear lady, that is not soon done! You and Mistress Anne, as you well know, first awoke me from my firm belief that I was none other than an elf, and yet there have since been times when I have doubted whether it were not indeed the truth.'

'Nay, Peregrine, at years of discretion you should have outgrown old wives' tales.'

'Better be an elf at once—a soulless creature of the elements—than the sport of an evil spirit doomed to perdition,' he bitterly exclaimed.

'Hush, hush! You know not what you are saying!'

'I know it too well, madam! There are times when I long and wish after goodness— nay, when Heaven seems open to me—and I resolve and strive after a perfect life; but again comes the wild, passionate dragging, as it were, into all that at other moments I most loathe and abhor, and I become no more my own master. Ah!'

There was misery in his voice, and he

clutched the long hair on each side of his face with his hands.

'St. Paul felt the same,' said Mrs. Woodford gently.

'"Who shall deliver me from the body of this death?" Ay, ay! how many times have I not groaned that forth! And so, if that Father at Turin were right, I am but as Paul was when he was Saul. Madam, is it not possible that I was never truly baptized?' he cried eagerly.

'Impossible, Peregrine. Was not Mr. Horncastle chaplain when you were born? Yes; and I have heard my brother say that both he and your father held the same views as the Church upon baptism.'

'So I thought; but Father Geronimo says that at the best it was but heretical baptism, and belike hastily and ineffectually performed.'

'Put that aside, Peregrine. It is only a temptation and allurement.'

'It is an allurement you know not how strong,' said the poor youth. 'Could I only bring myself to believe all that Father Geronimo does, and fall down before his Madonnas and saints, then could I hope for a new nature, and scourge away the old'—he set his teeth as he spoke—'till naught remains of the elf or demon, be it what it will.'

'Ah, Peregrine, scourging will not do it, but grace will, and that grace is indeed yours, as is proved by these higher aspirations.'

'I tell you, madam, that if I live on as I am doing now, grace will be utterly stifled, if it ever abode in me at all. Every hour that I live, pent in by intolerable forms and immeasurable dulness, the maddening temper gains on me! Nay, I have had to rush out at night and swear a dozen round oaths before I could compose myself to sit down to the endless supper. Ah, I shock you, madam! but that's not the worst I am driven to do.'

'Nor the way to bring the better spirit, my poor youth. Oh, that you would pray instead of swearing!'

'I cannot pray at Oakwood. My father and Mr. Horncastle drive away all the prayers that ever were in me, and I mean nothing, even though I keep my word to you.'

'I am glad you do that. While I know

you are doing so, I shall still believe the better angel will triumph.'

'How can aught triumph but hatred and disgust where I am pinned down? Listen, madam, and hear if good spirits have any chance. We break our fast, ere the sun is up, on chunks of yesterday's half-dressed beef and mutton. If I am seen seeking for a morsel not half raw, I am rated for dainty French tastes; and the same with the sour smallest of beer. I know now what always made me ill-tempered as a child, and I avoid it, but at the expense of sneers on my French breeding, even though my drink be fair water; for wine, look you, is a sinful expense, save for after dinner, and frothed chocolate for a man is an invention of Satan. The meal is sauced either with blame of me, messages from the farm-folk, or Bob's exploits in the chase. Then my father goes his rounds on the farm, and would fain have me with him to stand knee-deep in mire watching the plough, or feeling each greasy and odorous old sheep in turn to see if it be ready for the knife, or gloating over the bullocks or swine, or exchanging auguries with Thomas Vokes on this or that crop. Faugh! And I am told I shall never be good for a country gentleman if I contemn such matters! I say I have no mind to be a country gentleman, whereby I am told of Esau till I am sick of his very name.'

'But surely you have not always to follow on this round?'

'Oh no! I may go out birding with Bob, who is about as lively as an old jackass, or meet the country boobies for a hunt, and be pointed at as the Frenchman, and left to ride alone; or there's mine own chamber, when the maids do not see fit to turn me out with their pails and besoms, as they do at least twice a week—I sit there in my cloaks and furs (by the way, I am chidden for an effeminate fop if ever I am seen in them). I would give myself to books, as my uncle counselled, but what think you? By ill hap Bob, coming in to ask some question, found me studying the *Divina Commedia* of Dante Alighieri, and hit upon one of the engravings representing the torments of purgatory. What must he do but report it, and immediately a hue and cry arises that I am being corrupted with

Popish books. In vain do I tell them that their admirable John Milton, the only poet save Sternhold and Hopkins that my father deems not absolute pagan, knew, loved, and borrowed from Dante. All my books are turned over as ruthlessly as ever Don Quixote's by the curate and the barber, and whatever Mr. Horncastle's erudition cannot vouch for is summarily handed over to the kitchen wench to light the fires. The best of it is that they have left me my classics, as though old Terence and Lucan were lesser heathens than the great Florentine. However, I have bribed the young maid, and rescued my Dante and Boiardo with small damage, but I dare not read them save with door locked.'

Mrs. Woodford could scarcely shake her head at the disobedience, and she asked if there were really no other varieties.

'Such as fencing with that lubber Robert, and trying to bend his stiff limbs to the noble art of *l'escrime*. But that is after-dinner work. There is the mountain of half-raw flesh to be consumed first, and then my father, with Mr. Horncastle and Bob, discuss on what they call the news—happy if a poor rogue has been caught by Tom Constable stealing faggots. 'Tis argument for a week—almost equal to the price of a fat mutton at Portsmouth. My father and the minister nod in due time over their ale-cup, and Bob and I go our ways till dark, or till the house bell rings for prayers and exposition. Well, dear good lady, I will not grieve you by telling you how often they make me wish to be again the imp devoid of every shred of self-respect, and too much inured to flogging to heed what my antics might bring on me.'

'I am glad you have that shred of self-respect; I hope indeed it is some higher respect.'

'Well, I can never believe that Heaven meant to be served by mortal dulness. Seven years have only made old Horncastle blow his horn to the same note, only more drearily.'

'I can see indeed that it is a great trial to one used to the life of foreign Courts and to interest in great affairs like you, my poor Peregrine; but what can I say but to entreat you to be patient, try to find interest, and endeavour to win your father's confidence so that he may accord you more liberty? Did I not hear that your attention made your mother's life happier?'

Peregrine laughed. 'My mother! She has never seen aught but boorishness all her life, and any departure therefrom seems to her unnatural. I believe she is as much afraid of my courtesy as ever she was of my mischief, and that in her secret heart she still believes me a changeling. No, Madam Woodford, there is but one way to save me from the frenzy that comes over me.'

'Your father has already been entreated to let you join your uncle.'

'I know it—I know it; but if it were impossible before, that discovery of Dante has made it *impossibilissimo*, as the Italian would say, to deal with him now. There is a better way. Give me the good angel who has always counteracted the evil one. Give me Mistress Anne!'

'Anne, my Anne!' exclaimed Mrs. Woodford in dismay. 'O Peregrine, it cannot be!'

'I knew that would be your first word,' said Peregrine, 'but verily, madam, I would not ask it but that I know that I should be another man with her by my side, and that she would have nothing to fear from the evil that dies at her approach.'

'Ah, Peregrine! you think so now; but no man can be sure of himself with any mere human care. Besides, my child is not of degree to match with you. Your father would justly be angered if we took advantage of your attachment to us to encourage you in an inclination he could never approve.'

'I tell you, madam—yes, I must tell you all—my madness and my ruin will be completed if I am left to my father's will. I know what is hanging over me. He is only waiting till I am of age—at Midsummer, and the year of mourning is over for poor Oliver —I am sure no one mourns for him more heartily than I—to bind me to Martha Browning. If she would only bring the plague, or something worse than smallpox, to put an end to it at once!'

'But that would make any such scheme all the more impossible.'

'Listen, madam; do but hear me. Even as children the very sight of Martha Browning's solemn face'—Peregrine drew his countenance down into a portentous length—' her horror at the slightest word or sport, her stiff broomstick carriage, all impelled me to the most impish tricks. And now—letting alone that pock-marks have seamed her grim face till she is as ugly as Alecto—she is a Precisian of the Precisians. I declare our household is in her eyes sinfully free! If she can hammer out a text of Scripture, and write her name in characters as big and gawky as herself, 'tis as far as her education has carried her, save in pickling, preserving, stitchery, and clear-starching, the only arts not sinful in her eyes. If I am to have a broomstick, I had rather ride off on one at once to the Witches' sabbath on the Wartburg than be tied to one for life.'

'I should think she would scarce accept you.'

'There's no such hope. She has been bred up to regard one of us as her lot, and she would accept me without a murmur if I were Beelzebub himself, horns and tail and all! Why, she ogles me with her gooseberry eyes already, and treats me as a chattel of her own.'

'Hush, hush, Peregrine! I cannot have you talk thus. If your father had such designs, it would be unworthy of us to favour you in crossing them.'

'Nay, madam, he hath never expressed them as yet. Only my mother and brother both refer to his purpose, and if I could show myself contracted to a young lady of good birth and education, he cannot gainsay ; it might yet save me from what I will not and cannot endure. Not that such is by any means my chief and only motive. I have loved Mistress Anne with all my heart ever since she shone upon me like a being from a better world when I lay sick here. She has the same power of hushing the wild goblin within me as you have, madam. I am another man with her, as I am with you. It is my only hope! Give me that hope, and I shall be able to endure patiently.——Ah! what have I done? Have I said too much?'

He had talked longer and more eagerly than would have been good for the invalid even if the topic had been less agitating, and the emotion caused by this unexpected complication, consternation at the difficulties she foresaw, and the present difficulty of framing a reply, were altogether too much for Mrs. Woodford. She turned deadly white, and gasped for breath, so that Peregrine, in terror, dashed off in search of the maids, exclaiming that their mistress was in a swoon.

The Doctor came out of his study much distressed, and in Anne's absence the household was almost helpless in giving the succours in which she had always been the foremost. Peregrine lingered about in remorse and despair, offering to fetch her or to go for the doctor, and finally took the latter course, thereto impelled by the angry words of the old cook, an enemy of his in former days.

'No better? no, sir, nor 'tis not your fault if ever she be. You've been and frought her nigh to death with your terrifying ways.'

Peregrine was Hampshire man enough to know that to terrify only meant to tease, but he was in no mood to justify himself to old Patience, so he galloped off to Portsmouth, and only returned with the doctor to hear that Madam Woodford was in bed, and her daughter with her. She was somewhat better, but still very ill, and it was plain that this was no moment for pressing his suit even had it not been time for him to return home. Going to fetch the doctor might be accepted as a valid reason for missing the evening exhortation and prayer, but there were mistrustful looks that galled him.

Anne's return was more beneficial to Mrs. Woodford than the doctor's visit, and the girl was still too ignorant of all that her mother's attacks of spasms and subsequent weakness implied to be as much alarmed as to depress her hopes. Yet Mrs. Woodford, lying awake in the night, detected that her daughter was restless and unhappy, and asked what ailed her, and how the visit had gone off.

'You do not wish me to speak of such things, madam,' was the answer.

'Tell me all that is in your heart, my child.'

It all came out with the vehemence of a reserved nature when the flood is loosed. 'Young Madam' had been more than usually peevish and exacting, jealous perhaps at

Lucy's being the heroine of the day, and fretful over a cold which confined her to the house, how she worried and harassed all around her with her whims, megrims and complaints could only too well be imagined, and how the entire pleasure of the day was destroyed. Lucy was never allowed a minute's conversation with her friend without being interrupted by a whine and complaints of unkindness and neglect.

Lady Archfield's ill-usage, as the young wife was pleased to call every kind of restriction, was the favourite theme next to the daughter-in-law's own finery, her ailments, and her notions of the treatment befitting her.

And young Mr. Archfield himself, while handing his old friend out to the carriage that had fetched her, could not help confiding to her that he was nearly beside himself. His mother meant to be kind, but expected too much from one so brought up, and his wife—what could be done for her? She made herself miserable here, and every one else likewise. Yet even if his father would consent, she was utterly unfit to be mistress of a house of her own; and poor Charles could only utter imprecations on the guardians who could have had no idea how a young woman ought to be brought up. It was worse than an ill-trained hound.

Mrs. Woodford heard what she extracted from her daughter with grief and alarm, and not only for her friends.

'Indeed, my dear child,' she said, 'you must prevent such confidences. They are very dangerous things respecting married people.'

'It was all in a few moments, mamma, and I could not stop him. He is so unhappy;' and Anne's voice revealed tears.

'The more reason why you should avoid hearing what he will soon be very sorry you have heard. Were he not a mere lad himself, it would be as inexcusable as it is imprudent thus to speak of the troubles and annoyances that often beset the first year of wedded life. I am sorry for the poor youth, who means no harm nor disloyalty, and is only treating you as his old companion and playmate; but he has no right thus to talk of his wife, above all to a young maiden too inexperienced to counsel him, and if he should attempt to do so again, promise me, my daughter, that you will silence him—if by no other means, by telling him so.'

'I promise!' said Anne, choking back her tears and lifting her head. 'I am sure I never want to go to Fareham again while that Lieutenant Sedley Archfield is there. If those be army manners, they are what I cannot endure. He is altogether mean and hateful, above all when he scoffs at Master Oakshott.'

'I am afraid a great many do so, child, and that he often gives some occasion,' put in Mrs. Woodford, a little uneasy that this should be the offence.

'He is better than Sedley Archfield, be he what he will, madam,' said the girl. 'He never pays those compliments, those insolent disgusting compliments, such as he—that Sedley, I mean—when he found me alone in the hall, and I had to keep him at bay from trying to kiss me, only Mr. Archfield— Charley—came down the stairs before he was aware, and called out, "I will thank you to behave yourself to a lady in my father's house." And then he, Sedley, sneered "The Parson's niece!" with such a laugh, mother, I shall never get it out of my ears. As if I were not as well born as he!'

'That is not quite the way to take it, my child. I had rather you stood on your maidenly dignity and discretion than on your birth. I trust he will soon be away.'

'I fear he will not, mamma, for I heard say the troop are coming down to be under the Duke of Berwick at Portsmouth.'

'Then, dear daughter, it is the less mishap that you should be thus closely confined by loving attendance on me. Now, goodnight. Compose yourself to sleep, and think no more of these troubles.'

Nevertheless mother and daughter lay long awake, side by side, that night; the daughter in all the flutter of nerves induced by offended yet flattered feeling—hating the compliment, yet feeling that it was a compliment to the features that she was beginning to value. She was substantially a good, well-principled maiden, modest and discreet, with much dignified reserve, yet it was impossible that she should not have seen heads turned to look at her in Portsmouth, and know that she was admired above her contemporaries, so that even if it brought her inconvenience it was agreeable. Besides, her heart was beating with pity for the Archfields. The elder ones might have only themselves to blame, but it was very hard for poor Charles to have been blindly coupled to a being who did not know how to value him, still harder that there should be blame for a confidence where neither meant any harm— blame that made her blush on her pillow with indignant shame.

Perhaps Mrs. Woodford divined these thoughts, for she too meditated deeply on the perils of her fair young daughter, and in the morning could not leave her room. In the course of the day she heard that Master Peregrine Oakshott had been to inquire for her, and was not surprised when her brother-in-law sought an interview with her. The gulf between the hierarchy and squirearchy was sufficient for a marriage to be thought a *mesalliance*, and it was with a smile at the folly as well as with a certain displeased pity that Dr. Woodford mentioned the proposal so vehemently pressed upon him by Peregrine Oakshott for his niece's hand.

'Poor boy!' said Mrs. Woodford, 'it is a great misfortune. You forbade him of course to speak of such a thing.'

'I told him that I could not imagine how he could think us capable of entertaining any such proposal without his father's consent. He seems to have hoped that to pledge himself to us might extort sanction from his father, not seeing that it would be a highly improper measure, and would only incense the Major.'

'All the more that the Major wishes to pass on Mistress Martha Browning to him, poor fellow.'

'He did not tell me so.'

Mrs. Woodford related what he had said to her, and the Doctor could not but observe: 'The poor Major! his whole treatment of that unfortunate youth is as if he were resolved to drive him to distraction. But even if the Major were ever so willing, I doubt whether Master Peregrine be the husband you would choose for our little maid.'

'Assuredly not, poor fellow! though if she

loved him as he loves her—which happily she does not—I should scarce dare to stand in the way, lest she should be the appointed instrument for his good.'

'He assured me that he had never directly addressed her.'

'No, and I trust he never will. Not that she is ever like to love him, although she does not shrink from him quite as much as others do. Yet there is a strain of ambition in my child's nature that might make her seek the elevation. But, my good brother, for this and other reasons we must find another home for my poor child when I am gone. Nay, brother, do not look at me thus; you know as well as I do that I can scarcely look to see the spring come in, and I would fain take this opportunity of speaking to you concerning my dear daughter. No one can be a kinder father to her than you, and I would most gladly leave her to cheer and tend you, but as things stand around us she can scarce remain here without a mother's watchfulness. She is guarded now by her strict attendance on my infirmity, but when I am gone how will it be?'

'She is as good and discreet a maiden as parent could wish.'

'Good and discreet as far as her knowledge and experience go, but that is not enough. On the one hand, there is a certain wild temper about that young Master Oakshott such as makes me never know what he might attempt if, as he says, his father should drive him to desperation, and this is a lonely place, with the sea close at hand.'

'Lady Archfield would gladly take charge of her.'

Mrs. Woodford here related what Anne had said of Sedley's insolence, but this the Doctor thought little of, not quite believing in the regiment coming into the neighbourhood, and Mrs. Woodford most unwillingly was forced to mention her further unwillingness that her daughter should be made a party to the troubles caused by the silly young wife of her old playfellow.

'What more?' said the Doctor, holding up his hands. 'I never thought a discreet young maid could be such a care, but I suppose that is the price we pay for her good looks. Three of them, eh? What is it that you propose?'

'I should like to place her in the household of some godly and kindly lady, who would watch over her and probably provide for her marriage. That, as you know, was my own course, and I was very happy in Lady Sandwich's family, till I made the acquaintance of your dear and honoured brother, and my greater happiness began. The first day that I am able I will write to some of my earlier friends, such as Mrs. Evelyn and Mrs. Pepys, and again there is Mistress Eleanor Wall, who, I hear, is married to Sir Theophilus Oglethorpe, and who might accept my daughter for my sake. She is a warm, loving, open-hearted creature of Irish blood, and would certainly be kind to her.'

There was no indignity in such a plan. Most ladies of rank or quality entertained one or more young women of the clerical or professional classes as companions, governesses, or ladies' maids, as the case might be. They were not classed with the servants, but had their share of the society and amusements of the house, and a fair chance of marriage in their own degree, though the comfort of their situation varied a good deal according to the amiability of their mistress, from that of a confidential friend to a white slave and *souffre douleur*.

Dr. Woodford had no cause to object except his own loss of his niece's society and return to bachelor life, after the eight years of companionship which he had enjoyed; but such complications as were induced by the presence of an attractive young girl were, as he allowed, beyond him, and he acquiesced with a sigh in the judgment of the mother, whom he had always esteemed so highly.

The letters were written, and in due time received kind replies. Mrs. Evelyn proposed that the young gentlewoman should come and stay with her till some situation should offer itself, and Lady Oglethorpe, a warm-hearted Irishwoman, deeply attached to the Queen, declared her intention of speaking to the King or the Princess Anne on the first opportunity of the daughter of the brave Captain Woodford. There might very possibly be a nursery appointment to be had either at the Cockpit or at Whitehall in the course of the year.

This was much more than Mrs. Woodford had desired. She had far rather have placed her daughter immediately under some kind matronly lady in a private household; but she knew that her good friend was always eager to promise to the utmost of her possible power. She did not talk much of this to her daughter, only telling her that the kind ladies had promised to befriend her, and find a situation for her; and Anne was too much shocked to find her mother actually making such arrangements to enter upon any inquiries. The perception that her mother was looking forward to passing away so soon entirely overset her; she would not think about it, would not admit the bare idea of the loss. Only there lurked at the bottom of her heart the feeling that when the crash had come, and desolation had overtaken her, it would be more dreary at Portchester than anywhere else; and there might be infinite possibilities beyond for the King's godchild, almost a knight's daughter.

The next time that Mrs. Woodford heard

that Major Oakshott was at the door inquiring for her health, she begged as a favour that he would come and see her.

The good gentleman came upstairs treading gently in his heavy boots, as one accustomed to an invalid chamber.

'I am sorry to see you thus, madam,' he said, as she held out her wasted hand and thanked him. 'Did you desire spiritual consolations? There are times when our needs pass far beyond prescribed forms and ordinances.'

'I am thankful for the prayers of good men,' said Mrs. Woodford; 'but for truth's sake I must tell you that this was not foremost in my mind when I begged for this favour.'

He was evidently disappointed, for he was producing from his pocket the little stout black-bound Bible, which, by a dent in one of the lids, bore witness of having been with him in his campaigns; and perhaps half-diplomatically, as well as with a yearning for oneness of spirit, she gratified him by requesting him to read and pray.

With all his rigidity he was too truly pious

a man for his ministrations to contain anything in which, Churchwoman as she was, she could not join with all her heart, and feel comforting; but ere he was about to rise from his knees she said, 'One prayer for your son, sir.'

A few fervent words were spoken on behalf of the wandering sheep, while tears glistened in the old man's eyes, and fell fast from those of the lady, and then he said, 'Ah, madam! have I not wrestled in prayer for my poor boy?'

'I am sure you have, sir. I know you have a deep fatherly love for him, and therefore I sent to speak to you as a dying woman.'

'And I will gladly hear you, for you have always been good to him, and, as I confess, have done him more good—if good can be called the apparent improvement in one unregenerate—than any other.'

'Except his uncle,' said Mrs. Woodford. 'I fear it is vain to say that I think the best hope of his becoming a good and valuable man, a comfort and not a sorrow to yourself, would be to let him even now rejoin Sir Peregrine.'

'That cannot be, madam. My brother has not kept to the understanding on which I entrusted the lad to him, but has carried him into worldly and debauched company, such as has made the sober and godly habits of his home distasteful to him, and has further taken him into Popish lands, where he has become infected with their abominations to a greater extent than I can yet fathom.'

Mrs. Woodford sighed and felt hopeless. 'I see your view of the matter, sir. Yet may I suggest that it is hard for a young man to find wholesome occupation such as may guard him from temptation on an estate where the master is active and sufficient like yourself?'

'Protection from temptation must come from within, madam,' replied the Major; 'but I so far agree with you that in due time, when he has attained his twenty-first year, I trust he will be wedded to his cousin, a virtuous and pious young maiden, and will have the management of her property, which is larger than my own.'

'But if—if—sir, the marriage were distasteful to him, could it be for the happiness and welfare of either?'

'The boy has been complaining to you? Nay, madam, I blame you not. You have ever been the boy's best friend according to knowledge; but he ought to know that his honour and mine are engaged. It is true that Mistress Martha is not a Court beauty, such as his eyes have unhappily learnt to admire, but I am acting verily for his true good. "Favour is deceitful, and beauty is vain."'

'Most true, sir; but let me say one more word. I fear, I greatly fear, that all young spirits brook not compulsion.'

'That means, they will not bow their stiff necks to the yoke.'

'Ah, sir! but on the other hand, "Fathers, provoke not your children to wrath." Forgive me, sir; I spoke but out of true affection to your son, and the fear that what may seem to him severity may not drive him to some extremity that might grieve you.'

'No forgiveness is needed, madam. I thank you for your interest in him, and for your plain speaking according to your lights. I can but act according to those vouchsafed unto me.'

'And we both agree in praying for his true good,' said Mrs. Woodford.

And with a mutual blessing they parted, Mrs. Woodford deeply sorry for both father and son, for whom she had done what she could.

It was her last interview with any one outside the house. Another attack of spasms brought the end, during the east winds of March, so suddenly as to leave no time for farewells or last words. When she was laid to rest in the little churchyard within the castle walls, no one showed such overwhelming tokens of grief as Peregrine Oakshott, who lingered about the grave after the Doctor had taken his niece home, and was found lying upon it late in the evening, exhausted with weeping.

Yet Sedley Archfield, whose regiment had, after all, been sent to Portsmouth, reported that he had spent the very next afternoon at a cock-fight, ending in a carouse with various naval and military officers at a tavern, not drinking, but contributing to the mirth by foreign songs, tricks, and jests.

CHAPTER XII

THE ONE HOPE

> 'There's some fearful tie
> Between me and that spirit world, which God
> Brands with His terrors on my troubled mind.'
>
> KINGSLEY.

THE final blow had fallen upon Anne Woodford so suddenly that for the first few days she moved about as one in a dream. Lady Archfield came to her on the first day, and showed her motherly kindness, and Lucy was with her as much as was possible under the exactions of young madam, who was just sufficiently unwell to resent attention being paid to any other living creature. She further developed a jealousy of Lucy's affection for any other friend such as led to a squabble between her and her husband, and made her mother-in-law unwillingly acquiesce in the expediency of Anne's being farther off.

And indeed Anne herself felt so utterly forlorn and desolate that an impatience of the place came over her. She was indeed fond of her uncle, but he was much absorbed in his studies, his parish, and in anxious correspondence on the state of the Church, and was scarcely a companion to her, and without her mother to engross her love and attention, and cut off from the Archfields as she now was, there was little to counterbalance the restless feeling that London and the precincts of the Court were her natural element. So she wrote her letters according to her mother's desire, and waited anxiously for the replies, feeling as if anything would be preferable to her present unhappiness and solitude.

The answers came in due time. Mrs. Evelyn promised to try to find a virtuous and godly lady who would be willing to receive Mistress Anne Woodford into her family, and Lady Oglethorpe wrote with vaguer promises of high preferment, which excited Anne's imagination during those lonely hours that she had to spend while her strict mourning, after the custom of the time, secluded her from all visitors.

Meantime, in that anxious spring of 1688, when the Church of England was looking to her defences, the Doctor could not be much at home, and when he had time to listen to private affairs, he heard reports which did not please him of Peregrine Oakshott. That the young men in the county all abhorred his fine foreign airs was no serious evil, though it might be suspected that his sharp ironical tongue had quite as much to do with their dislike as his greater refinement of manner.

His father was reported to be very seriously displeased with him, for he openly expressed contempt of the precise ways of the household, and absented himself in a manner that could scarcely be attributed to aught but the licentious indulgences of the time; and as he seldom mingled in the amusements of the young country gentlemen, it was only too probable that he found a lower grade of companions in Portsmouth. Moreover his talk, random though it might be, offended all the Whig opinions of his father. He talked with the dogmatism of the traveller of the glories of Louis XIV, and broadly avowed his views that the grandeur of the nation was best established under a king who asked no questions of people or Parliament, 'that senseless set of chattering pies,' as he was reported to have called the House of Commons.

He sang the praises of the gracious and graceful Queen Mary Beatrice, and derided 'the dried-up Orange stick,' as he called the hope of the Protestants; nor did he scruple to pronounce Popery the faith of chivalrous gentlemen, far preferable to the whining of sullen Whiggery. No one could tell how far all this was genuine opinion, or simply delight in contradiction, especially of his father, who was in a constant state of irritation at the son whom he could so little manage.

And in the height of the wrath of the whole of the magistracy at the expulsion of their lord-lieutenant, the Earl of Gainsborough, and the substitution of the young Duke of Berwick, what must Peregrine do but argue in high praise of that youth, whom he had several times seen and admired. And when not a gentleman in the neighbourhood chose to greet the intruder when he arrived as governor of Portsmouth, Peregrine actually rode in to see him, and dined with him. Words cannot express the Major's anger and shame at such consorting with a person, whom alike, on account of parentage, religion, and education, he regarded as a son of perdition. Yet Peregrine would only coolly reply that he knew many a Protestant who would hardly compare favourably with young Berwick.

It was an anxious period that spring of 1688. The order to read the King's Declaration of Indulgence from the pulpit had come as a thunderclap upon the clergy. The English Church had only known rest for twenty-eight years, and now, by this unconstitutional assumption of prerogative, she seemed about to be given up to be the prey of Romanists on the one hand and Nonconformists on the other; though for the present the latter were so persuaded that the Indulgence was merely a disguised advance of Rome that they were not at all grateful, expecting, as Mr. Horncastle observed, only to be the last devoured, and he was as much determined as was Dr. Woodford not to announce it from his pulpit, whatever might be the consequence; the latter thus resigning all hopes of promotion.

News letters, public and private, were eagerly scanned. Though the diocesan, Bishop Mew, took no active part in the petition called a libel, being an extremely aged man, the imprisonment of Ken, so deeply endeared to Hampshire hearts when Canon of Winchester and Rector of Brighstone, and with the Bloody Assize and the execution of Alice Lisle fresh in men's memories, there could not but be extreme anxiety.

In the midst arrived the tidings that a son had been born to the King—a son instantly baptized by a Roman Catholic priest, and no doubt destined by James to rivet the fetters of Rome upon the kingdom, destroying at once the hope of his elder sister's accession. Loyal Churchmen like the Archfields still hoped, recollecting how many infants had been born in the Royal Family only to die; but at Oakwood the Major and his chaplain shook their heads, and spoke of warming pans, to the vehement displeasure of Peregrine, who was sure to respond that the

Queen was an angel, and that the Whigs credited every one with their own sly tricks.

The Major groaned, and things seemed to have reached a pass very like open enmity between father and son, though Peregrine still lived at home, and reports were rife that the year of mourning for his brother being expired, he was, as soon as he came of age, to be married to Mistress Martha Browning, and have an establishment of his own at Emsworth.

Under these circumstances, it was with much satisfaction that Dr. Woodford said to his niece: 'Child, here is an excellent offer for you. Lady Russell, who you know has returned to live at Stratton, has heard you mentioned by Lady Mildmay. She has just married her eldest daughter, and needs a companion to the other, and has been told of you as able to speak French and Italian, and otherwise well trained. What! do you not relish the proposal?'

'Why, sir, would not my entering such a house do you harm at Court, and lessen your chance of preferment?'

'Think not of *that*, my child.'

'Besides,' added Anne, 'since Lady Oglethorpe has written, it would not be fitting to engage myself elsewhere before hearing from her again.'

'You think so, Anne. Lady Russell's would be a far safer, better home for you than the Court.'

Anne knew it, but the thought of that widowed home depressed her. It might, she thought, be as dull as Oakwood, and there would be infinite chances of preferment at Court. What she said, however, was: 'It was by my mother's wish that I applied to Lady Oglethorpe.'

'That is true, child. Yet I cannot but believe that if she had known of Lady Russell's offer, she would gladly and thankfully have accepted it.'

So said the secret voice within the girl herself, but she did not yet yield to it. 'Perhaps she would, sir,' she answered, 'if the other proposal were not made. 'Tis a Whig household though.'

'A Whig household is a safer one than a Popish one,' answered the Doctor. 'Lady Russell is, by all they tell me, a very saint upon earth.'

Shall it be owned? Anne thought of Oakwood, and was not attracted towards a saint upon earth. 'How soon was the answer to be given?' she asked.

'I believe she would wish you to meet her at Winchester next week, when, if you pleased her, you might return with her to Stratton.'

The Doctor hoped that Lady Oglethorpe's application might fail, but before the week was over she forwarded the definite appointment of Mistress Anne Jacobina Woodford as one of the rockers of his Royal Highness the Prince of Wales, his Majesty having been graciously pleased to remember her father's services and his own sponsorship. 'If your friends consider the office somewhat beneath you,' wrote Lady Oglethorpe, 'it is still open to you to decline it.'

'Oh no; I would certainly not decline it!' cried Anne. 'I could not possibly do so; could I, sir?'

'Lady Oglethorpe says you might,' returned the Doctor; 'and for my part, niece, I should prefer the office of a *gouvernante* to that of a rocker.'

'Ah, but it is to a Prince!' said Anne. 'It is the way to something further.'

'And what may that something further be? That is the question,' said her uncle. 'I will not control you, my child, for the application to this Court lady was by the wish of your good mother, who knew her well, but I own that I should be far more at rest on your account if you were in a place of less temptation.'

'The Court is very different from what it was in the last King's time,' pleaded Anne.

'In some degree it may be; but on the other hand, the influence which may have purified it is of the religion that I fear may be a seduction.'

'Oh no, never, uncle; nothing could make me a Papist.'

'Do not be over-confident, Anne. Those who run into temptation are apt to be left to themselves.'

'Indeed, sir, I cannot think that the course my mother shaped for me can be a running into temptation.'

'Well, Anne, as I say, I cannot withstand you, since it was your mother who requested

Lady Oglethorpe's patronage for you, though I tell you sincerely that I believe that had the two courses been set before her she would have chosen the safer and more private one.'

'Nay but, dear sir,' still pleaded the maiden, 'what would become of your chances of preferment if it were known that you had placed me with Lord Russell's widow in preference to the Queen?'

'Let not that weigh with you one moment, child. I believe that no staunch friend of our Protestant Church will be preferred by his Majesty; nay, while the Archbishop and my saintly friend of Bath and Wells are persecuted, I should be ashamed to think of promotion. Spurn the thought from you, child.'

'Nay, 'twas only love for you, dear uncle.'

'I know it, child. I am not displeased, only think it over, and pray over it, since the post will not go out until to-morrow.'

Anne did think, but not quite as her uncle intended. The remembrance of the good-natured young Princesses, the large stately rooms, the brilliant dresses, the radiance of wax lights, had floated before her eyes ever since her removal from Chelsea to the quieter regions of Winchester, and she had longed to get back to them. She really loved her uncle, and whatever he might say, she longed to push his advancement, and thought his unselfish abnegation the greater reason for working for him; and in spite of knowing well that it was only a dull back-stair appointment, she could look to the notice of Princess Anne, when once within her reach, and further, with the confidence of youth, believed that she had that within her which would make her way upwards, and enable her to confer promotion, honour, and dignity, on all her friends. Her uncle should be a Bishop, Charles a Peer (fancy his wife being under obligations to the parson's niece!), Lucy should have a perfect husband, and an appointment should be found for poor Peregrine which his father could not gainsay. It was her bounden duty not to throw away such advantages; besides loyalty to her Royal godfather could not permit his offer to be rejected, and her mother, when writing to Lady Oglethorpe, must surely have had some such expectation. Nor should she be entirely cut off from her uncle, who was a Royal chaplain ; and this was some consolation to the good Doctor when he found her purpose fixed, and made arrangements for her to travel up to town in company with Lady Worsley of Gatcombe, whom she was to meet at Southampton on the 1st of July.

Meantime the Doctor did his best to arm his niece against the allurements to Romanism that he feared would be held out. Lady Oglethorpe and other friends had assured him of the matronly care of Lady Powys and Lady Strickland to guard their department from all evil; but he did fear these religious influences, and Anne, resolute to resist all, perhaps not afraid of the conflict, was willing to arm herself for defence, and listened readily. She was no less anxious to provide for her uncle's comfort in his absence, and many small matters of housewifery that had stood over for some time were now to be purchased, as well as a few needments for her own outfit, although much was left for the counsel of her patroness in the matter of garments.

Accordingly her uncle rode in with her to

Portsmouth on a shopping expedition, and as the streets of the seaport were scarcely safe for a young woman without an escort, he carried a little book in his pocket wherewith he beguiled the time that she spent in the selection of his frying-pans, fire-irons, and the like, and her own gloves and kerchiefs. They dined at the 'ordinary' at the inn, and there Dr. Woodford met his great friends Mr. Stanbury of Botley, and Mr. Worsley of Gatcombe, in the Isle of Wight, who both, like him, were opposed to the reading of the Declaration of Indulgence, as unconstitutional, and deeply anxious as to the fate of the greatly beloved Bishop of Bath and Wells. It was inevitable that they should fall into deep and earnest council together, and when dinner was over they agreed to adjourn to the house of a friend learned in ecclesiastical law to hunt up the rights of the case, leaving Anne to await them in a private room at the Spotted Dog, shown to her by the landlady.

Anne well knew what such a meeting betided, and with a certain prevision, had armed herself with some knotting, wherewith she sat down in a bay window overlooking the street, whence she could see market-women going home with empty baskets, pigs being reluctantly driven down to provision ships in the harbour, barrels of biscuit, salt meat, or beer, being rolled down for the same purpose, sailors in loose knee-breeches, and soldiers in tall peaked caps and cross-belts, and officers of each service moving in different directions. She sat there day-dreaming, feeling secure in her loneliness, and presently saw a slight figure, daintily clad in gray and black, who catching her eye made an eager gesture, doffing his plumed hat and bowing low to her. She returned his salute, and thought he passed on, but in another minute she was startled to find him at her side, exclaiming: 'This is the occasion I have longed and sought for, Mistress Anne ; I bless and thank the fates.'

'I am glad to see you once more before I depart,' said Anne, holding out her hand as frankly as she could to the old playfellow whom she always thought ill-treated, but whom she could never meet without a certain shudder.

'Then it is true?' he exclaimed.

'Yes; I am to go up with Lady Worsley from Southampton next week.'

'Ah!' he cried, 'but must that be?' and she felt his strange power, so that she drew into herself and said haughtily—

'My dear mother wished me to be with her friends, nor can the King's appointment be neglected, though of course I am extremely grieved to go.'

'And you are dazzled with all these gewgaws of Court life, no doubt?'

'I shall not be much in the way of gewgaws just yet,' said Anne drily. 'It will be dull enough in some back room of Whitehall or St. James's.'

'Say you so. You will wish yourself back—you, the lady of my heart—mine own good angel! Hear me. Say but the word, and your home will be mine, to say nothing of your own most devoted servant.'

'Hush, hush, sir! I cannot hear this,' said Anne, anxiously glancing down the street in hopes of seeing her uncle approaching.

'Nay, but listen! This is my only hope —my only chance—I must speak—you doom me to you know not what if you will not hear me!'

'Indeed, sir, I neither will nor ought!'

'Ought! Ought! Ought you not to save a fellow-creature from distraction and destruction? One who has loved and looked to you ever since you and that saint your mother lifted me out of the misery of my childhood.'

Then as she looked softened he went on: 'You, you are my one hope. No one else can lift me out of the reach of the demon that has beset me even since I was born.'

'That is profane,' she said, the more severe for the growing attraction of repulsion.

'What do I care? It is true! What was I till you and your mother took pity on the wild imp? My old nurse said a change would come to me every seven years. That blessed change came just seven years ago. Give me what will make a more blessed— a more saving change—or there will be one as much for the worse.'

'But—I could not. No! you must see

for yourself that I could not—even if I would,' she faltered, really pitying now, and unwilling to give more pain than she could help.

'Could not? It should be possible. I know how to bring it about. Give me but your promise, and I will make you mine—ay, and I will make myself as worthy of you as man can be of saint-like maid.'

'No—no! This is very wrong—you are pledged already——'

'No such thing—believe no such tale. My promise has never been given to that grim hag of my father's choice—no, nor should be forced from me by the rack. Look you here. Let me take this hand, call in the woman of the house, give me your word, and my father will own his power to bind me to Martha is at an end.'

'Oh no! It would be a sin — never. Besides——' said Anne, holding her hands tightly clasped behind her in alarm, lest against her will she should let them be seized, and trying to find words to tell him how little she felt disposed to trust her heart and herself to one whom she might indeed pity, but with a sort of shrinking as from something

not quite human. Perhaps he dreaded her
'besides'—for he cut her short.

'It would save ten thousand greater sins.
See, here are two ways before us. Either
give me your word, your precious word, go
silent to London, leave me to struggle it out
with my father and your uncle and follow
you. Hope and trust will be enough to
bear me through the battle without, and
within deafen the demon of my nature,
and render me patient of my intolerable
life till I have conquered and can bring you
home.'

Her tongue faltered as she tried to say
such a secret unsanctioned engagement would
be treachery, but he cut off the words.

'You have not heard me out. There is
another way. I know those who will aid me.
We can meet in early dawn, be wedded in
one of these churches in all secrecy and haste.
and I would carry you at once to my uncle,
who, as you well know, would welcome you
as a daughter. Or, better still, we would to
those fair lands I have scarce seen, but where
I could make my way with sword or pen with
you to inspire me. I have the means. My

uncle left this with me. Speak! It is death or life to me.'

This last proposal was thoroughly alarming, and Anne retreated, drawing herself to her full height, and speaking with the dignity that concealed considerable terror.

'No, indeed, sir. You ought to know better than to utter such proposals. One who can make such schemes can certainly obtain no respect nor regard from the lady he addresses. Let me pass'—for she was penned up in the bay window—'I shall seek the landlady till my uncle returns.'

'Nay, Mistress Anne, do not fear me. Do not drive me to utter despair. Oh, pardon me! Nothing but utter desperation could drive me to have thus spoken; but how can I help using every effort to win her whose very look and presence is bliss! Nothing else soothes and calms me; nothing else so silences the demon and wakens the better part of my nature. Have you no pity upon a miserable wretch, who will be dragged down to his doom without your helping hand?'

He flung himself on his knee before her, and tried to grasp her hand.

'Indeed, I am sorry for you, Master Oakshott,' said Anne, compassionate, but still retreating as far as the window would let her; 'but you are mistaken. If this power be in me, which I cannot quite believe—yes, I see what you want to say, but if I did what I know to be wrong, I should lose it at once; God's grace can save you without me.'

'I will not ask you to do what you call wrong; no, nor to transgress any of the ties you respect, you whose home is so unlike mine; only tell me that I may have hope, that if I deserve you, I may win you; that you could grant me—wretched me—a share of your affection.'

This was hardest of all; mingled pity and repugnance, truth and compassion strove within the maiden as well as the strange influence of those extraordinary eyes. She was almost as much afraid of herself as of her suitor. At last she managed to say, 'I am very sorry for you; I grieve from my heart for your troubles; I should be very glad to hear of your welfare, and anything good of you, but——'

'But, but—I see—it is mere frenzy in me

to think the blighted elf can aspire to be aught but loathsome to any lady—only, at least, tell me you love no one else.'

'No, certainly not,' she said, as if his eyes drew it forcibly from her.

'Then you cannot hinder me from making you my guiding star—hoping that if yet I can——'

'There's my uncle!' exclaimed Anne, in a tone of infinite relief. 'Stand up, Mr. Oakshott, compose yourself. Of course I cannot hinder your thinking about me, if it will do you any good, but there are better things to think about which would conquer evil and make you happy more effectually.'

He snatched her hand and kissed it, nor did she withhold it, since she really pitied him, and knew that her uncle was near, and all would soon be over.

Peregrine dashed away by another door as Dr. Woodford's foot was on the stairs. 'I have ordered the horses,' he began. 'They told me young Oakshott was here.'

'He was, but he is gone;' and she could not quite conceal her agitation.

'Crimson cheeks, my young mistress?

Ah, the foolish fellow! You do not care for him, I trust?'

'No, indeed, poor fellow. What, did you know, sir?'

'Know. Yes, truly—and your mother likewise, Anne. It was one cause of her wishing to send you to safer keeping than mine seems to be. My young spark made his proposals to us both, though we would not disturb your mind therewith, not knowing how he would have dealt with his father, nor viewing him, for all he is heir to Oakwood, as a desirable match in himself. I am glad to see you have sense and discretion to be of the same mind, my maid.'

'I cannot but grieve for his sad condition, sir,' replied Anne, 'but as for anything more —it would make me shudder to think of it— he is still too like Robin Goodfellow.'

'That's my good girl,' said her uncle. 'And do you know, child, there are the best hopes for the Bishops. There's a gentleman come down but now from London, who says 'twas like a triumph as the Bishops sat in their barge on the way to the Tower; crowds swarming along the banks, begging for their blessing, and they waving it with tears in their eyes. The King will be a mere madman if he dares to touch a hair of their heads. Well, when I was a lad, Bishops were sent to the Tower by the people; I little thought to live to see them sent thither by the King.'

All the way home Dr. Woodford talked of the trial, beginning perhaps to regret that his niece must go to the very focus of Roman influence in England, where there seemed to be little scruple as to the mode of conversion. Would it be possible to alter her destination? was his thought, when he rose the next day, but loyalty stood in the way, and that very afternoon another event happened which made it evident that the poor girl must leave Portchester as soon as possible.

She had gone out with him to take leave of some old cottagers in the village, and he finding himself detained to minister to a case of unexpected illness, allowed her to go home alone for about a quarter of a mile along the white sunny road at the foot of Portsdown, with the castle full in view at one end, and the cottage where he was at the other. Many

a time previously had she trodden it alone,
but she had not reckoned on two officers
coming swaggering from a cross road down
the hill, one of them Sedley Archfield, who
immediately called out, 'Ha, ha! my pretty
maid, no wench goes by without paying toll;'
and they spread their arms across the road so
as to arrest her.

'Sir,' said Anne, drawing herself up with
dignity, 'you mistake——'

'Not a whit, my dear; no exemption
here;' and there was a horse laugh, and an
endeavour to seize her, as she stepped back,
feeling that in quietness lay her best chance
of repelling them, adding—

'My uncle is close by.'

'The more cause for haste;' and they
began to close upon her. But at that moment
Peregrine Oakshott, leaping from his horse,
was among them, with the cry—

'Dastards! insulting a lady.'

'Lady, forsooth! the parson's niece.'

In a few seconds—very long seconds to
her—her flying feet had brought her back
to the cottage, where she burst in with—
'Pardon, pardon, sir; come quick; there are

swords drawn; there will be bloodshed if you do not come.'

He obeyed the summons without further query, for when all men wore swords the neighbourhood of a garrison was only too liable to such encounters outside. There was no need for her to gasp more; from the very cottage door he could see the need of haste, for the swords were actually flashing, and the two young men in position to fight. Anne shook her head, unable to do more than sign her thanks to the good woman of the cottage, who offered her a seat. She leant against the door, and watched as her uncle, sending his voice before him, called on them to desist.

There was a start, then each drew back and held down his weapon, but with a menacing gesture on one side, a shrug of the shoulders on the other, which impelled the Doctor to use double speed in the fear that the parting might be with a challenge reserved.

He was in time to stand warning, and arguing that if he pardoned the slighting words and condoned the insult to his niece, no one had a right to exact vengeance ; and in truth, whatever were his arguments, he so dealt with the two young men as to force them into shaking hands before they separated, though with a contemptuous look on either side—a scowl from Sedley, a sneer from Peregrine, boding ill for the future, and making him sigh.

'Ah! sister, sister, you judged aright. Would that I could have sent the maid sooner away rather than that all this ill blood should have been bred. Yet I may only be sending her to greater temptation and danger. But she is a good maiden ; God bless her and keep her here and there, now and for evermore, as I trust He keepeth our good Dr. Ken in this sore strait. The trial may even now be over. Ah, my child, here you are! Frightened were you by that rude fellow ? Nay, I believe you were almost equally terrified by him who came to the rescue. You will soon be out of their reach, my dear.'

'Yes, that is one great comfort in going,' sighed Anne. One comfort—yes—though she would not have stayed had the choice been given her now. And shall the thought be told that flashed over her and coloured her cheeks with a sort of shame yet of pleasure, 'I surely must have power over men! I know mother would say it is a terrible danger one way, and a great gift another. I will not misuse it; but what will it bring me? Or am I only a rustic beauty after all, who will be nobody elsewhere?'

Still heartily she wished that her rescuer had been any one else in the wide world. It was almost uncanny that he should have sprung out of the earth at such a moment.

CHAPTER XIII

THE BONFIRE

'From Eddystone to Berwick bounds,
  From Lynn to Milford Bay,
That time of slumber was as
  Bright and busy as the day :
For swift to east and swift to west
  The fiery herald sped,
High on St. Michael's Mount it shone :
  It shone on Beachy Head.'
                    MACAULAY.

DR. WOODFORD and his niece had not long reached their own door when the clatter of a horse's hoofs was heard, and Charles Archfield was seen, waving his hat and shouting 'Hurrah!' before he came near enough to speak.

'Good news, I see!' said the Doctor.

'Good news indeed! Not guilty! Express rode from Westminster Hall with the news at ten o'clock this morning. All acquitted.

Expresses could hardly get away for the hurrahing of the people. Hurrah! hurrah! hurrah!' cried the young man, throwing up his hat, while Dr. Woodford, taking off his own, gave graver, deeper thanks that justice was yet in England, that these noble and honoured confessors were safe, and that the King had been saved from further injustice and violence to the Church.

'We are to have a bonfire on Portsdown Hill,' added Charles. 'They will be all round the country, in the Island, and everywhere. My father is rid one way to spread the tidings, and give orders. I'm going on into Portsmouth, to see after tar barrels. You'll be there, sir, and you, Anne?' There was a moment's hesitation after the day's encounters, but he added, 'My mother is going, and my little Madam, and Lucy. They will call for you in the coach if you will be at Ryder's cottage at nine o'clock. It will not be dark enough to light up till ten, so there will be time to get a noble pile ready. Come, Anne, 'tis Lucy's last chance of seeing you—so strange as you have made yourself of late.'

This plea decided Anne, who had been on

the point of declaring that she should have an excellent view from the top of the keep. However, not only did she long to see Lucy again, but the enthusiasm was contagious, and there was an attraction in the centre of popular rejoicing that drew both her and her uncle, nor could there be a doubt of her being sufficiently protected when among the Archfield ladies. So the arrangement was accepted, and then there was the cry—

'Hark! the Havant bells! Ay! and the Cosham! Portsmouth is pealing out. That's Alverstoke. They know it there. A salute! Another.'

'Scarce loyal from the King's ships,' said the Doctor smiling.

'Nay, 'tis only loyalty to rejoice that the King can't make a fool of himself. So my father says,' rejoined Charles.

And that seemed to be the mood of all England. When Anne and her uncle set forth in the summer sunset light the great hill above them was dark with the multitudes thronging around the huge pyre rising in the midst. They rested for some minutes at the cottage indicated before the arrival of Sir

Philip, who rode up accompanying the coach in which his three ladies were seated, and which was quite large enough to receive Dr. Woodford and Mistress Anne. Charles was in the throng, in the midst of most of the younger gentlemen of the neighbourhood, and a good many of the naval and military officers, directing the arrangement of the pile.

What a scene it was, as seen even from the windows of the coach where the ladies remained, for the multitude of sailors, soldiers, town and village people, though all unanimous, were far too tumultuous for them to venture beyond their open door, especially as little Mrs. Archfield was very far from well, and nothing but her eagerness for amusement could have brought her hither, and of course she could not be left. Probably she knew as little of the real bearings of the case or the cause of rejoicing as did the boys who pervaded everything with their squibs, and were only restrained from firing them in the faces of the horses by wholesome fear of the big whips of the coachman and outriders who stood at the horses' heads.

It was hardly yet dark when the match

was put to the shavings, and to the sound of the loud 'Hurrahs!' and cries of 'Long live the Bishops!' 'Down with the Pope!' the flame kindled, crackled, and leapt up, while a responsive fire was seen on St. Catherine's Down in the Isle of Wight, and northward, eastward, westward, on every available point, each new light greeted by fresh acclamations, as it shone out against the summer night sky, while the ships in the harbour showed their lights, reflected in the sea, as the sky grew darker. Then came a procession of sailors and other rough folk, bearing between poles a chair with a stuffed figure with a kind of tiara, followed by others with scarlet hats and capes, and with reiterated shouts of 'Down with the Pope!' these were hurled into the fire with deafening hurrahs, their more gorgeous trappings being cleverly twitched off at the last moment, as part of the properties for the 5th of November.

Little Mrs. Archfield clapped her hands and screamed with delight as each fresh blaze shot up, and chattered with all her might, sometimes about some lace and perfumes which she wanted Anne to procure for her in

London at the sign of the Flower Pot, sometimes grumbling at her husband having gone off to the midst of the party closest to the fire, ' Just like Mr. Archfield, always leaving her to herself,' but generally very well amused, especially when a group of gentlemen, officers, and county neighbours gathered round the open door talking to the ladies within.

Peregrine was there with his hands in his pockets, and a queer ironical smile writhing his features. He was asked if his father and brother were present.

'Not my father,' he replied. 'He has a logical mind. Martha is up here with her guardian, and I am keeping out of her way, and my brother is full in the thick of the fray. A bonfire is a bonfire to most folks, were it to roast their grandsire!'

'Oh, fie, Master Oakshott, how you do talk!' laughed Mrs. Archfield.

'Nay, but you rejoice in the escape of the good Bishops,' put in Lucy.

'For what?' asked Peregrine. 'For refusing to say live and let live?'

'Not against letting *live*, but against saying so unconstitutionally, my young friend,' said

Dr. Woodford, 'or tyrannising over our consciences.'

Generally Peregrine was more respectful to Dr. Woodford than to any one else; but there seemed to be a reckless bitterness about him on that night, and he said, 'I marvel with what face those same Right Reverend Seigniors will preach against the French King.'

'Sir,' thrust in Sedley Archfield, 'I am not to hear opprobrious epithets applied to the Bishops.'

'What was the opprobrium?' lazily demanded Peregrine, and in spite of his unpopularity, the laugh was with him. Sedley grew more angry.

'You likened them to the French King——'

'The most splendid monarch in Europe,' said Peregrine coolly.

'A Frenchman!' quoth one of the young squires with withering contempt.

'He has that ill fortune, sir,' said Peregrine. 'Mayhap he would be sensible of the disadvantage, if he evened himself with some of my reasonable countrymen.'

'Do you mean that for an insult, sir?' exclaimed Sedley Archfield, striding forward.

'As you please,' said Peregrine. 'To me it had the sound of compliment.'

'Oh la! they'll fight,' cried Mrs. Archfield. 'Don't let them! Where's the Doctor? Where's Sir Philip?'

'Hush, my dear,' said Lady Archfield; 'these gentlemen would not fall out close to us.'

Dr. Woodford was out of sight, having been drawn into controversy with a fellow-clergyman on the limits of toleration. Anne looked anxiously for him, but with provoking coolness Peregrine presently said, 'There's no crowd near, and if you will step out, the fires on the farther hills are to be seen well from the knoll hard by.'

He spoke chiefly to Anne, but even if she had not a kind of shrinking from trusting herself with him in this strange wild scene, she would have been prevented by Mrs. Archfield's eager cry—

'Oh, I'll come, let me come! I'm so weary of sitting here. Thank you, Master Oakshott.'

Lady Archfield's remonstrance was lost as Peregrine helped the little lady out, and there was nothing for it but to follow her, as close as might be, as she hung on her cavalier's arm chattering, and now and then giving little screams of delight or alarm. Lady Archfield and her daughter each was instantly squired, but Mistress Woodford, a nobody, was left to keep as near them as she could, and gaze at the sparks of light of the beacons in the distance, thinking how changed the morrow would be to her.

Presently a figure approached, and Charles Archfield's voice said, 'Is that you, Anne? Did I hear my wife's voice?'

'Yes, she is there.'

'And with that imp of evil! I would his own folk had him!' muttered Charles, dashing forward with ' How now, madam? you were not to leave the coach!'

She laughed exultingly. 'Ha, sir! see what comes of leaving me to better cavaliers, while you run after your fire! I should have seen nothing but for Master Oakshott.'

'Come with me now,' said Charles; 'you ought not to be standing here in the dew.'

'Ha, ha! what a jealous master,' she said; but she put her arm into his, saying with a courtesy, 'Thank you, Master Oakshott, lords must be obeyed. I should have been still buried in the old coach but for you.'

Peregrine fell back to Anne. 'That blaze is at St. Helen's,' he began. 'That—what! will you not wait a moment?'

'No, no! They will want to be going home.'

'And have you forgotten that it is only just over Midsummer? This is the week of my third seventh—the moment for change. O Anne! make it a change for the better. Say the word, and the die will be cast. All is ready! Come!'

He tried to take her hand, but the vehemence of his words, spoken under his breath, terrified her, and with a hasty 'No, no! you know not what you talk of,' she hastened after her friends, and was glad to find herself in the safe haven of the interior of the coach.

Ere long they drove down the hill, and at the place of parting were set down, the last words in Anne's ears being Mrs. Archfield's injunctions not to forget the orange flower-water at the sign of the Flower Pot, drowning Lucy's tearful farewells.

As they walked away in the moonlight a figure was seen in the distance.

'Is that Peregrine Oakshott?' asked the Doctor. 'That young man is in a desperate mood, ready to put a quarrel on any one. I hope no harm will come of it.'

CHAPTER XIV

GATHERING MOUSE-EAR

'I heard the groans, I marked the tears.
I saw the wound his bosom bore.'
SCOTT.

AFTER such an evening it was not easy to fall asleep, and Anne tossed about, heated, restless, and uneasy, feeling that to remain at home was impossible, yet less satisfied about her future prospects, and doubtful whether she had not done herself harm by attending last night's rejoicings, and hoping that nothing would happen to reveal her presence there.

She was glad that the night was not longer, and resolved to take advantage of the early morning to fulfil a commission of Lady Oglethorpe, whose elder children, Lewis and Theophilus, had the whooping-cough. Mouse-ear, namely, the little sulphur-coloured hawk-weed, was, and still is, accounted a specific, and Anne had been requested to bring a supply—a thing easily done, since it grew plentifully in the court of the castle.

She dressed herself in haste, made some of her preparations for the journey, and let herself out of the house, going first for one last look at her mother's green grave in the dewy churchyard, and gathering from it a daisy, which she put into her bosom, then in the fair morning freshness, and exhilaration of the rising sun, crossing the wide tilt-yard, among haycocks waiting to be tossed, and arriving at the court within, filling her basket between the churchyard and the gateway tower and keep, when standing up for a moment she was extremely startled to see Peregrine Oakshott's unmistakable figure entering at the postern of the court.

With vague fears of his intentions, and instinctive terror of meeting him alone, heightened by that dread of his power, she flew in at the great bailey tower door, hoping that he had not seen her, but tolerably secure that even if he had, and should pursue her, she was sufficiently superior in knowledge of the stairs and passages to baffle him, and make her way along the battlements to the tower at the corner of the court nearest the parsonage, where there was a turret stair by which she could escape.

Up the broken stairs she went, shutting behind her every available door in the chambers and passages, but not as quickly as she wished, since attention to her feet was needful in the ruinous state of steps and walls. Through these massive walls she could hear nothing distinctly, but she fancied voices and a cry, making her seek more intricate windings, nor did she dare to look out till she had gained a thick screen of bushy ivy at the corner of the turret, where a little door opened on the broad summit of the battlemented wall.

Then, what horror was it that she beheld? Or was it a dream? She even passed her hands over her face and looked again. Peregrine and Charles, yes, it was Charles Archfield, were fighting with swords in the court beneath. She gave a shriek, in a wild hope of parting them, but at that instant she saw

Peregrine fall, and with the impulse of rushing to aid she hurried down, impeded, however, by stumbles, and by the doors she herself had shut, and when she emerged, she saw only Charles, standing like one dazed and white as death.

'O Mr. Archfield! where is he? What have you done?'

The young man pointed to the opening of the vault. Then, speaking with an effort, 'He was quite dead; my sword went through him. He forced it on me—he was pursuing you. I withstood him—and——'

He gasped heavily as the words came one by one. She trembled exceedingly, and would have looked into the vault, with, 'Are you quite sure?' but he grasped her hand and withheld her.

'Only too sure! Yes, I have done it! It could not be helped. I would give myself up at once, but, Anne, there is my wife. They tell me any shock would kill her as she is now. I should be double murderer. Will you keep the secret, Anne, always my friend? And 'twas for you.'

'Indeed, indeed, I will not betray you. I

go away in two hours,' said Anne ; and he caught her hand. 'But oh!' and she pointed to the blood on the grass, then with sudden thought, 'Heap the hay over it,' running to fill her arms with the lately-cut grass.

He mechanically did the same, and then they stood for a moment, awe-stricken.

'God forgive me!' said the poor young man. 'How to hide it I hardly know, but for *her* sake—ah, 'twas that brought me here. She could not rest last night till I had promised to be here early enough in the morning to give you a piece of sarcenet to be matched in London. Where is it? Ah! I forget. It seems to be ages ago that she was insisting that I should ride over so as to be in time.'

'Lucy must write,' said Anne. 'O Charley! wipe that dreadful sword ; look like yourself. I am going in a couple of hours. There is no fear of me! but oh! that you should have done such a thing! and through me!'

'Hush! hush! don't talk. I must be gone ere folks are about. My horse is outside.' He wrung her hand and kissed it, forgetting to give her the pattern, and Anne, still stunned, walked back to the parsonage, her one thought how to control herself so as to guard Charles's secret.

It must be remembered that in the generation succeeding that which had fought a long civil war, and when duels were common assertions of honour and self-respect among young gentlemen, homicide was not so exceptional and heinous an offence in ordinary eyes as when a higher value has come to be set on life, and acts of violence are far less frequent.

Charles had drawn his sword in fair fight, and in her own defence, and thus it was natural that Anne Woodford should think of his deed, certainly with a shudder, but with more of pity than of horror, and with gratitude that made her feel bound to do her utmost to guard him from the consequences; also there was a sense of relief, and perhaps a feeling as if the victim were scarcely a human creature like others. It never occurred to her till some time after to recollect it would have had an unpleasant sound that she had been the occasion of such an 'unseemly brawl' between two young men, one of them a married man. When the thought occurred to her it made the blood rush hotly to her cheeks.

It was well for her that the pain of leaving home and the bustle of preparation concealed that she had suffered a great shock, and accounted for her not being able to taste any breakfast beyond a draught of milk. Her ears were intent all the time to perceive any token whether the haymakers had come into the court and had discovered any trace of the ghastly thing in the vault, and she hardly heard the kind words of her uncle or the coaxings of his old housekeeper. She dreaded especially the sight of Hans, so fondly attached to his master's nephew, and it was with a sense of infinite relief—instead of the tender grief otherwise natural—that she was seated in the boat for Portsmouth, and her uncle believing her to be crying, left her undisturbed till she had composed herself to wear the front that she knew was needful, however her heart might throb beneath it, and as their boat threaded its way through the ships, even then numerous, she looked wistfully up at the tall tower of the castle, with earnest prayers for the living, and a longing she durst not utter, to ask her uncle whether it were right to pray for the poor strange, struggling soul, always so cruelly misunderstood, and now so summarily dismissed from the world of trial.

Yet presently there was a revulsion of feeling as she was roused from her meditations by the coxswain's answer to her uncle, who had asked what was a smart, swift little smack, which after receiving something from a boat, began stretching her wings and making all sail for the Isle of Wight.

The men looked significant and hesitated.

'Smugglers, eh? Traders in French brandy?' asked the Doctor.

'Well, your reverence, so they says. They be a rough lot out there by at the back of the Island.'

'There would be small harm in letting a poor man get a drink of spirits cheap to warm his heart,' said one of the other men; 'but they say as how 'tis a very nest of 'em out there, and that's how no one can ever pitch on the highwaymen, such as robbed Farmer Vine t'other day a-coming home from market.'

'They do say,' added the other, 'that there's them as ought to know better that is thick with them. There's that young master up at Oakwood—that crooked slip as they used to say was a changeling—gets out o' window o' nights and sails with them.'

'He has nought to do with the robberies, they say,' added the coxswain; 'but I could tell of many a young spark who has gone out with the fair traders for the sport's sake, and because gentle folk don't know what to do with their time.'

'And they do say the young chap is kept uncommon tight at home.'

Here the sight of a vessel of war coming in changed the topic, but it had given Anne something more to think of. Peregrine had spoken of means arranged for making her his own. Could that smuggling yacht have anything to do with them? He could hardly have reckoned on meeting her alone in the morning, but he might have attempted to find her thus—or failing that, he might have run down the boat. If so, she had a great deliverance to be thankful for, and Charles's timely appearance had been a great blessing.

But Peregrine! poor Peregrine! it became doubly terrible that he should have perished on the eve of such a deed. It was cruel to entertain such thoughts of the dead, yet it was equally impossible not to feel comfort in being rid for ever of one who had certainly justified the vague alarm which he had always excited in her. She could not grieve for him now that the first shock was over, but she must suppress all tokens of her extreme anxiety on account of Charles Archfield.

Thus she was landed at Portsmouth, and walked up the street to the Spotted Dog, where Lady Worsley was taking an early noonchine before starting for London, having crossed from the little fishing village of Ryde. Here Anne parted with her uncle, who promised an early letter, though she could hardly restrain a shudder at the thought of the tidings that it might contain.

CHAPTER XV

NEWS FROM FAREHAM

'My soul its secret hath, my life too hath its mystery.
Hopeless the evil is, I have not told its history.'
JEAN INGELOW.

LADY WORSLEY was a handsome, commanding old dame, who soon made her charge feel the social gulf between a county magnate and a clergyman's niece. She decidedly thought that Mistress Anne Jacobina held her head too high for her position, and was, moreover, conceited of an unfortunate amount of good looks.

Therefore the good lady did her best to repress these dangerous tendencies by making the girl sit on the back seat with two maids, and uttering long lectures on humility, modesty, and discretion which made the blood of the sea captain's daughter boil with indignation.

Yet she always carried with her the dread of being pursued and called upon to accuse Charles Archfield of Peregrine's death. It was a perpetual cloud, dispersed, indeed, for a time by the events of the day, but returning at night, when not only was the combat acted over again, but when she fell asleep it was only to be pursued by Peregrine through endless vaulted dens of darkness, or, what was far worse, to be trying to hide a stream of blood that could never be stanched.

It was no wonder that she looked pale in the morning, and felt so tired and dejected as to make her sensible that she was cast loose from home and friends when no one troubled her with remarks or inquiries such as she could hardly have answered. However, when, on the evening of the second day's journey, Anne was set down at Sir Theophilus Oglethorpe's house at Westminster, she met with a very different reception.

Lady Oglethorpe, a handsome, warm-hearted Irishwoman, met her at once in the hall with outstretched hands, and a kiss on each cheek.

'Come in, my dear, my poor orphan, the daughter of one who was very dear to me! Ah, how you have grown! I could never have thought this was the little Anne I recollect. You shall come up to your chamber at once, and rest you, and make ready for supper, by the time Sir Theophilus comes in from attending the King.'

Anne found herself installed in a fresh-smelling wainscotted room, where a glass of wine and some cake was ready for her, and where she made herself ready, feeling exhilarated in spirits as she performed her toilet, putting on her black evening dress, and refreshing the curls of her brown hair. It was a simple dress of deep mourning, but it became her well, and the two or three gentlemen who had come in to supper with Sir Theophilus evidently admired her greatly, and complimented her on having a situation at Court, which was all that Lady Oglethorpe mentioned.

'Child,' she said afterwards, when they were in private, 'if I had known what you looked like I would have sought a different position for you. But, there, to get one's foot—were it but the toe of one's shoe—in at Court is the great point after all, the rest must come after. I warrant me you are well educated too. Can you speak French?'

'Oh yes, madam, and Italian, and dance and play on the spinnet. I was with two French ladies at Winchester every winter who taught such things.'

'Well, well, mayhap we may get you promoted to a sub-governess's place—though your religion is against you. You are not a Catholic—eh?'

'No, your ladyship.'

'That's the only road to favour nowadays, though for the name of the thing they may have a Protestant or two. You are the King's godchild too, so he will expect it the more from you. However, we may find a better path. You have not left your heart in the country, eh?'

Anne blushed and denied it.

'You will be mewed up close enough in the nursery,' ran on Lady Oglethorpe. 'Lady Powys keeps close discipline there, and I expect she will be disconcerted to see how fine a fish I have brought to her net; but we will see—we will see how matters go. But, my dear, have you no coloured clothes? There is no appearing in the Royal household in private mourning. It might daunt the Prince's spirits in his cradle!' and she laughed, though Anne felt much annoyed at thus disregarding her mother, as well as at the heavy expense. However, there was no help for it; the gowns and laces hidden in the bottom of her mails were disinterred, and the former were for the most part condemned, so that she had to submit to a fresh outfit, in which Lady Oglethorpe heartily interested herself, but which drained the purse that the Canon had amply supplied.

These arrangements were not complete when the first letter from home arrived, and was opened with a beating heart, and furtive glances as of one who feared to see the contents, but they were by no means what she expected.

I hope you have arrived safely in London, and that you are not displeased with your first taste of life in a Court. Neither town nor country is exempt from sorrow and death. I was summoned only on the second day after your departure to share in the sorrows at Archfield, where the poor young wife died early on Friday morning, leaving a living infant, a son, who, I hope, may prove a blessing to them, if he is spared, which can scarcely be expected. The poor young man, and indeed all the family, are in the utmost distress, and truly there were circumstances that render the event more than usually deplorable, and for which he blames himself exceedingly, even to despair. It appears that the poor young gentlewoman wished to add some trifle to the numerous commissions with which she was entrusting you on the night of the bonfire, and that she could not be pacified except by her husband undertaking to ride over to give the patterns and the orders to you before your setting forth. You said nothing of having seen him—nor do I see how it was possible that you could have done so, seeing that you only left your chamber just before the breakfast that you never tasted, my poor child. He never returned till long after noon, and what with fretting after him, and disappointment, that happened which Lady Archfield had always apprehended, and the poor fragile young creature worked herself into a state which ended before midnight in the birth of a puny babe, and her own death shortly after. She wanted two months of completing her sixteenth year, and was of so frail a constitution that Dr. Brown had never much hope of her surviving the birth of her child. It was a cruel thing to marry her thus early, ungrown in body or mind, but she had no one to care for her before she was brought hither. The blame, as I tell Sir Philip, and would fain persuade poor Charles, is really with those who bred her up so uncontrolled as to be the victim of her humours; but the unhappy youth will listen to no consolation. He calls himself a murderer, shuts himself up, and for the most part will see and speak to no one, but if forced by his father's command to unlock his chamber door, returns at once to sit with his head hidden in his arms crossed upon the table, and if father, mother, or sister strive to rouse him and obtain answer from him, he will only murmur forth, 'I should only make it worse if I did.' It is piteous to see a youth so utterly overcome, and truly I think his condition is a greater distress to our good friends than the loss of the poor young wife. They asked him what name he would have given to his child, but all the answer they could get was, 'As you will, only not mine;' and in the enforced absence of my brother of Fareham I baptized him Philip. The funeral will take place to-morrow, and Sir Philip proposes immediately after to take his son to Oxford, and there endeavour to find a tutor of mature age and of prudence, with whom he may either study at New College or be sent on the grand tour. It is the only notion that the poor lad has seemed willing to entertain, as if to get away from his misery, and I cannot but think it well for him. He is not yet twenty, and may, as it were, begin life again the wiser and the better man for his present extreme sorrow. Lady Archfield is greatly wrapped up in the care of the babe, who, I fear, is in danger of being killed by overcare, if by nothing else, though truly all is in the hands of God. I have scarce quitted the afflicted family since I was summoned to them on Friday, since Sir Philip has no one else on whom to depend for comfort or counsel; and if I can obtain the services of Mr. Ellis from Portsmouth for a few Sundays, I shall ride with him to Oxford to assist in the choice of a tutor to go abroad with Mr. Archfield.

One interruption, however, I had, namely, from Major Oakshott, who came in great perturbation to ask what was the last I had seen of his son Peregrine. It appears that the unfortunate young man never returned home after the bonfire on Portsdown Hill, where his brother Robert lost sight of him, and after waiting as long as he durst, returned home alone. It has become known that after parting with us high words passed between him and Lieutenant Sedley Archfield, insomuch that after the unhappy fashion of these times blood was demanded, and early in the morning Sedley sent the friend who was to act as second to bear the challenge to young Oakshott. You can conceive the reception that he was likely to receive at Oakwood; but it was then discovered that Peregrine had not been in his bed all night, nor had any one seen or heard of him. Sedley boasts loudly that the youngster has fled the country for fear of him, and truly things have that appearance, although to my mind Peregrine was far from wanting in spirit or courage. But, as he had not received the cartel, he might not have deemed his honour engaged to await it, and I incline to the belief that he is on his way to his uncle in Muscovy, driven thereto by his dread of the marriage with the gentlewoman whom he holds in so much aversion. I have striven to console his father by the assurance that such tidings of him will surely arrive in due time, but the Major is bitterly grieved, and is galled by the accusation of cowardice. 'He could not even be true to his own maxims of worldly honour,' says the poor gentleman. 'So true it is that only by grace we stand fast.' The which is true enough, but the poor gentleman unwittingly did his best to make grace unacceptable in his son's eyes. I trust soon to hear again of you, my dear child. I rejoice that Lady Oglethorpe is so good to you, and I hope that in the palace you will guard first your faith and then your discretion. And so praying always for your welfare, alike spiritual and temporal.—Your loving uncle,

JNO. WOODFORD.

Truly it was well that Anne had secluded herself to read this letter.

So the actual cause for which poor Charles Archfield had entreated silence was at an end. The very evil he had apprehended had come to pass, and she could well understand how, on his return in a horror-stricken, distracted state of mind, the childish petulance of his wife had worried him into loss of temper, so that he hardly knew what he said. And what must not his agony of remorse be? She could scarcely imagine how he had avoided confessing all as a mere relief to his mind, but then she reflected that when he called himself a murderer the words were taken in another sense, and no questions asked, nor would he be willing to add such grief and shame to his parents' present burthen, especially as no suspicion existed.

That Peregrine's fate had not been discovered greatly relieved her. She believed the vault to go down to a considerable depth after a first platform of stone near the opening, and it was generally avoided as the haunt of hobgoblins, fairies, or evil beings, so that no one was likely to be in its immediate neighbourhood after the hay was carried, so that there might have been nothing to attract any one to the near neighbourhood and thus lead to the discovery. If not made by this time, Charles would be far away, and there was nothing to connect him with the deed. No one save herself had even known of his having been near the castle that morning. How strange that the only persons aware of that terrible secret should be so far separated from one another that they could exchange no confidences; and each was compelled to absolute silence. For as long as no one else was suspected, Anne felt her part must be not to betray Charles, though the bare possibility of the accusation of another was agony to her.

She wrote her condolences in due form to Fareham, and in due time was answered by Lucy Archfield. The letter was full of details about the infant, who seemed to absorb her and her mother, and to be as likely to live as any child of those days ever was—and it was in his favour that his grandmother and her old nurse had better notions of management than most of her contemporaries. In spite of all that Lucy said of her brother's overwhelming grief, and the melancholy of thus parting with him, there was a strain of cheerfulness throughout the letter, betraying that the poor young wife of less than a year was no very great loss to the peace and comfort of the family. The letter ended with—

> There is a report that Sir Peregrine Oakshott is dead in Muscovy. Nothing has been heard of that unfortunate young man at Oakwood. If he be gone in quest of his uncle, I wonder what will become of him? However, nurse will have it that this being the third seventh year of his life, the fairies have carried off their changeling—you remember how she told us the story of his being changed as an infant, when we were children at Winchester; she believes it as much as ever, and never let little Philip out of her sight before he was baptized. I ask her, if the changeling be gone, where is the true Peregrine? but she only wags her head in answer.

A day or two later Anne heard from her uncle from Oxford. He was extremely grieved at the condition of his beloved *alma mater*, with a Roman Catholic Master reigning at University College, a doctor from the Sorbonne and Fellows to match, inflicted by military force on Magdalen, whose lawful children had been ejected with a violence beyond anything that the colleges had suffered even in the time of the Rebellion. If things went on as they were, he pronounced Oxford would be no better than a Popish seminary: and he had the more readily induced his old friend to consent to Charles's desire not to remain there as a student, but to go abroad with Mr. Fellowes, one of the expelled fellows of Magdalen, a clergyman of mature age, but a man of the world, who had already acted as a travelling tutor. Considering that the young widower was not yet twenty, and that all his wife's wealth would be in his hands, also that his cousin Sedley formed a dangerous link with the questionable diversions of the garrison at Portsmouth, both father and friend felt that it was well that he should be out of reach, and have other occupations for the present.

Change of scene had, Dr. Woodford said,

brightened the poor youth, and he was showing more interest in passing events, but probably he would never again be the lighthearted boy they used to know.

Anne could well believe it.

CHAPTER XVI

A ROYAL NURSERY

'The duty that I owe unto your Majesty
I seal upon the lips of this sweet babe.'
King Richard III.

It was not till the Queen had moved from St. James's, where her son had been born, to take up her abode at Whitehall, that Lady Oglethorpe was considered to be disinfected from her children's whooping-cough, and could conduct Mistress Anne Jacobina Woodford to her new situation.

Anne remembered the place from times past, as she followed the lady up the broad stairs to the state rooms, where the child was daily carried for inspection by the nation to whom, it was assumed, he was so welcome, but who, on the contrary, regarded him with the utmost dislike and suspicion.

Whitehall was, in those days, free to all the world, and though sentries in the Life-guards' uniform with huge grenadier caps were posted here and there, every one walked up and down. Members of Parliament and fine gentlemen in embroidered coats and flowing wigs came to exchange news; country cousins came to stare and wonder, some to admire, some to whisper their disbelief in the Prince's identity; clergy in gown, cassock, and bands came to win what they could in a losing cause; and one or two other clergy, who were looked at askance, whose dress had a foreign air, and whose tonsure could be detected as they threaded their way with quick, gliding steps to the King's closet.

Lady Oglethorpe, as one to the manner born, made her way through the midst of this throng in the magnificent gallery, and Anne followed her closely, conscious of words of admiration and inquiries who she was. Into the Prince's presence chamber, in fact his day-nursery, they came, and a sweet and gentle-looking lady met them, and embraced Lady Oglethorpe, who made known Mistress Woodford to Lady Strickland, of Sizergh, the second governess, as the fourth rocker who had been appointed.

'You are welcome, Miss Woodford,' said the lady, looking at Anne's high, handsome head and well-bred action in courtesying, with a shade of surprise. 'You are young, but I trust you are discreet. There is much need thereof.'

Following to a kind of alcove, raised by a step or two, Anne found herself before a half-circle of ladies and gentlemen round a chair of state, in front of which stood a nurse, with an infant in her arms, holding him to be caressed and inspected by the lady on the throne. Her beautiful soft dark eyes and hair, and an ivory complexion, with her dignified and graceful bearing, her long, slender throat and exquisite figure, were not so much concealed as enhanced by the simple mob cap and 'night-gown,' as it was then the fashion to call a morning wrapper, which she wore, and Anne's first impression was that no wonder Peregrine raved about her. Poor Peregrine! that very thought came like a stab, as, after courtesying low, she stood at the end of the long room—silent, and observing.

A few gentlemen waited by the opposite door, but not coming far into the apartment, and Lady Oglethorpe was announced by one of them. The space was so great that Anne could not hear the words, and she only saw the gracious smile and greeting as Lady Oglethorpe knelt and kissed the Queen's hand. After a long conversation between the mothers, during which Lady Oglethorpe was accommodated with a cushion, Anne was beckoned forward, and was named to the Queen, who honoured her with an inclination of the head and a few low murmured words.

Then there was an announcement of ' His Majesty,' and Anne, following the general example of standing back with low obeisances, beheld the tall active figure and dark heavy countenance of her Royal godfather, under his great black, heavily-curled wig. He returned Lady Oglethorpe's greeting, and his face lighted up with a pleasant smile that greatly changed the expression as he took his child into his arms for a few moments; but the little one began to cry, whereupon he was carried off, and the King began to consult Lady Oglethorpe upon the water-gruel on which the poor little Prince was being reared, and of which she emphatically disapproved.

Before he left the room, however, Lady Oglethorpe took care to present to him his god-daughter, Mistress Anne Jacobina Woodford, and very low was the girl's obeisance before him, but with far more fright and shyness than before the sweet-faced Queen.

'Oh ay!' he said, 'I remember honest Will Woodford. He did good service at Southwold. I wish he had left a son like him. Have you a brother, young mistress?'

'No, please your Majesty, I am an only child.'

'More's the pity,' he said kindly, and with a smile brightening his heavy features. ''Tis too good a breed to die out. You are Catholic?'

'I am bred in the English Church, so please your Majesty.'

His Majesty was evidently less pleased than before, but he only said, 'Ha! and my godchild! We must amend that,' and waved her aside.

The royal interview over, the newcomer

was presented to the State Governess, the Countess of Powys, a fair and gracious matron, who was, however, almost as far removed from her as the Queen. Then she was called on to take a solemn oath before the Master of the Household of dutiful loyalty to the Prince.

Mrs. Labadie was head nurse as well as being wife to the King's French valet. She was a kindly, portly Englishwoman, who seemed wrapped up in her charge, and she greeted her new subordinate in a friendly way, which, however, seemed strange in one who at home would have been of an inferior degree, expressed hopes of her steadiness and discretion, and called to Miss Dunord to show Miss Woodford her chamber. The abbreviation Miss sounded familiar and unsuitable, but it had just come into use for younger spinsters, though officially they were still termed Mistress.

Mistress or Miss Dunord was sallow and gray-eyed, somewhat older than Anne, and looking thoroughly French, though her English was perfect. She was entirely dressed in blue and white, and had a rosary and cross at her girdle. 'This way,' she said, tripping up a steep wooden stair. 'We sleep above. 'Tis a huge, awkward place. Her Majesty calls it the biggest and most uncomfortable palace she ever was in.'

Opening a heavy door, she showed a room of considerable size, hung with faded frayed tapestry, and containing two huge bedsteads, with four heavy posts, and canopies of wood, as near boxes as could well be. Privacy was a luxury not ordinarily coveted, and the arrangement did not surprise Anne, though she could have wished that on that summer day curtains and tapestry had been less fusty. Two young women were busy over a dress spread on one of the beds, and with French ease and grace the guide said, 'Here is our new colleague, Miss Jacobina Woodford. Let me present Miss Hester Bridgeman and Miss Jane Humphreys.'

'Miss Woodford is welcome,' said Miss Bridgeman, a keen, brown, lively, somewhat anxious-looking person, courtesying and holding out her hand, and her example was followed by Jane Humphreys, a stout, rosy, commonplace girl.

'Oh! I am glad,' this last cried. 'Now I shall have a bedfellow.'

This Anne was the less sorry for, as she saw that the bed of the other two was furnished with a holy water stoup and a little shrine with a waxen Madonna. There was only one looking-glass among the four, and not much apparatus either for washing or the toilet, but Miss Bridgeman believed that they would soon go to Richmond, where things would be more comfortable. Then she turned to consult Miss Dunord on her endeavour to improve the trimmings of a dress of Miss Humphreys.

'Yes, I know you are always in Our Lady's colours, Pauline, but you have a pretty taste, and can convince Jane that rose colour and scarlet cannot go together.'

'My father chose the ribbons,' said Jane, as if that were unanswerable.

'City taste,' said Miss Bridgeman.

'They are pretty, very pretty with anything else,' observed Pauline, with more tact. 'See, now, with your white embroidered petticoat and the gray train they are ravishing —and the scarlet coat will enliven the black.'

There was further a little murmur about what a Mr. Hopkins admired, but it was lost in the arrival of Miss Woodford's mails.

They clustered round, as eager as a set of schoolgirls, over Anne's dresses. Happily even the extreme of fashion had not then become ungraceful.

'Her Majesty will not have the loose drapery that folks used to wear,' said Hester Bridgeman.

'No,' said Pauline; 'it was all very well for those who could dispose it with an artless negligence, but for some I could name, it was as though they had tumbled it on with a hay-fork, and had their hair tousled by being tickled in the hay.'

'Now we have the tight bodice with plenty of muslin and lace, the gown open below to show the petticoat,' said Hester; 'and to my mind it is more decorous.'

'Decorum was not the vogue then,' laughed Pauline, 'perhaps it will be now. Oh, what lovely lace! real Flanders, on my word! Where did you get it, Miss Woodford?'

'It was my mother's.'

'And this? Why, 'tis old French point, you should hang it to your sleeves.'

'My Lady Archfield gave it to me in case I should need it.'

'Ah! I see you have good friends and are a person of some condition,' put in Hester Bridgeman. 'I shall be happy to consort with you. Let us——'

Anne courtesied, and at the moment a bell was heard, Pauline at once crossed herself and fell on her knees before the small shrine with a figure of the Blessed Virgin, and Hester, breaking off her words, followed her example; but Jane Humphreys stood twisting the corner of her apron.

In a very short time, almost before Anne had recovered from her bewilderment, the other two were up and chattering again.

'You are not a Catholic?' demanded Miss Bridgeman.

'I was bred in the Church,' said Anne.

'And you the King's godchild!' exclaimed Pauline. 'But we shall soon amend that and make a convert of you like Miss Bridgeman there.'

Anne shook her head, but was glad to

ask, 'And what means the bell that is ringing now?'

'That is the supper bell. It rings just after the Angelus,' said Hester. 'No, it is not ours. The great folks, Lady Powys, Lady Strickland, and the rest sup first. We have the dishes after them, with Nurses Labadie and Royer and the rest—no bad ones either. They are allowed five dishes and two bottles of wine apiece, and they always leave plenty for us, and it is served hot too.'

The preparations for going down to the second table now absorbed the party.

As Hester said, the fare at this second table was not to be despised. It was a formal meal shared with the two nurses and the two pages of the backstairs. Not the lads usually associated with the term, but men of mature age, and of gentle, though not noble, birth and breeding; and there were likewise the attendants of the King and Queen of the same grade, such as Mr. Labadie, the King's valet, some English, but besides these, Dusian, the Queen's French page, and Signor and Signora Turini, who had come with her from Modena, Père Giverlai, her confessor, and another priest. Père Giverlai said grace, and the conversation went on briskly between the elders, the younger ones being supposed to hold their peace.

Their dishes went in reversion to the inferior class of servants, laundress, sempstress, chambermaids, and the like, who had much more liberty than their betters, and not such a lack of occupation, as Anne soon perceived that she should suffer from.

There was, however, a great muster of all the Prince's establishment, who stood round, as many as could, with little garments in their hands, while he was solemnly undressed and laid in his richly inlaid and carved cradle —over which Père Giverlai pronounced a Latin benediction.

The nursery establishment was then released, except one of the nurses, who was to sleep or wake on a couch by his side, and one of the rockers. These damsels had, two at a time, to divide the night between them, one being always at hand to keep the food warm, touch the rocker at need with her foot, or call up the nurse on duty if the child awoke, but not presume herself to handle his little Royal Highness.

It was the night when Mistress Dunord and Bridgeman were due, and Anne followed Jane Humphreys to her room, asking a little about the duties of the morrow.

'We must be dressed before seven,' said the girl. 'One of us will be left on duty while the others go to Mass. I am glad you are a Protestant, Miss Woodford, for the Catholics put everything on me that they can.'

'We must do our best to help and strengthen each other,' said Anne.

'It is very hard,' said Jane; 'and the priests are always at me! I would change as Hester Bridgeman has done, but that I know it would break my grand-dame's heart. My father might not care so much, if I got advancement, but I believe it would kill my grandmother.'

'Advancement! oh, but faith comes first,' exclaimed Anne, recalling the warning.

'Hester says one religion is as good as another to get to Heaven by,' murmured Jane.

'Not if we deny our own for the world's

sake,' said Anne. 'Is the chapel here a Popish one?'

'No; the Queen has an Oratory, but the Popish chapel is at St. James's—across the Park. The Protestant one is here at Whitehall, and there are daily prayers at nine o'clock, and on Sunday music with three fiddlers, and my grandmother says it might almost as well be Popish at once.'

'Did your grandmother bring you up?'

'Yes. My mother died when I was seven years' old, and my grandmother bred us all up. You should hear her talk of the good old times before the Kings came back and there were no Bishops and no book prayers —but my father says we must swim with the stream, or he would not have got any custom at his coffee-house.'

'Is that his calling?'

'Ay! No one has a better set of guests than in the Golden Lamb. The place is full. The great Dr. Hammond sees his patients there, and it is all one buzz of the wits. It was because of that that my Lord Sunderland made interest, and got me here. How did you come?'

Anne briefly explained, and Jane broke out—

'Then you will be my friend, and we will tell each other all our secrets. You are a Protestant too. You will be mine, and not Bridgeman's or Dunord's—I hate them.'

In point of fact Anne did not feel much attracted by the proffer of friendship, and she certainly did not intend to tell Jane Humphreys all her secrets, nor to vow enmity to the other colleagues, but she gravely answered that she trusted they would be friends and help to maintain one another's faith. She was relieved that Miss Bridgeman here came in to take her first turn of rest till she was to be called up at one o'clock.

As Jane Humphreys had predicted, Mrs. Royer and Anne alone were left in charge of the nursling while every one went to morning Mass. Then followed breakfast and the levee of his Royal Higness, lasting as on the previous day till dinner-time; and the afternoon was as before, except that the day was fine enough for the child to be carried out with all his attendants behind him to take the air in the private gardens.

If this was to be the whole course of life at the palace, Anne began to feel that she had made a great mistake. She was by no means attracted by her companions, though Miss Bridgeman decided that she must know persons of condition, and made overtures of friendship, to be sealed by calling one another Oriana and Portia. She did not approve of such common names as Princess Anne and Lady Churchill used—Mrs. Morley and Mrs. Freeman! They must have something better than what was used by the Cockpit folks, and she was sure that her dear Portia would soon be of the only true faith.

CHAPTER XVII

MACHINATIONS

'Baby born to woe.'
F. T. PALGRAVE.

WHEN Anne Woodford began to wake from the constant thought of the grief and horror she had left at Portchester, and to feel more alive to her surroundings and less as if they were a kind of dream, in which she only mechanically took her part, one thing impressed itself on her gradually, and that was disappointment. If the previous shock had not blunted all her hopes and aspirations, perhaps she would have felt it sooner and more keenly; but she could not help realising that she had put herself into an inferior position whence there did not seem to be the promotion she had once anticipated. Her

companion rockers were of an inferior grade
to herself. Jane Humphreys was a harmless
but silly girl, not much wiser, though less
spoilt, than poor little Madam, and full of
Cockney vulgarities. Education was un-
fashionable just then, and though Hester
Bridgeman was better born and bred, being
the daughter of an attorney in the city, she
was not much better instructed, and had no
pursuits except that of her own advantage.
Pauline Dunord was by far the best of the
three, but she seemed to live a life apart,
taking very little interest in her companions
or anything around her except her devotions
and the bringing them over to her Church.
The nursery was quite a separate establishment; there was no mingling with the guests
of royalty, who were only seen in excited
peeps from the window, or when solemnly
introduced to the presence chamber to pay
their respects to the Prince. As to books,
the only secular one that Anne saw while at
Whitehall was an odd volume of *Parthenissa*.
The late King's summary of the Roman controversy was to be had in plenty, and nothing
was more evident than that the only road to

favour or promotion was in being thereby convinced.

'Don't throw it down as if it were a hot chestnut,' said her Oriana. 'That's what they all do at first, but they come to it at last.'

Anne made no answer, but a pang smote her as she thought of her uncle's warnings. Yet surely she might hope for other modes of prospering, she who was certainly by far the best looking and best educated of all the four, not that this served her much in her present company, and those of higher rank did not notice her at all. Princess Anne would surely recollect her, and then she might be safe in a Protestant household, where her uncle would be happy about her.

The Princess had been at Bath when first she arrived, but at the end of a week preparations were made at the Cockpit, a sort of appendage to Whitehall, where the Prince and Princess of Denmark lived, and in due time there was a visit to the nursery. Standing in full ceremony behind Lady Powys, Anne saw the plump face and form she recollected in the florid bloom of a young matron, not without a certain royal dignity in the pose

of the head, though in grace and beauty far
surpassed by the tall, elegant figure and face
of Lady Churchill, whose bright blue eyes
seemed to be taking in everything everywhere. Anne's heart began to beat high at
the sight of a once familiar face, and with
hopes of a really kind word from one who as
an elder girl had made much of the pretty
little plaything. The Princess Anne's countenance was, however, less good-natured than
usual; her mouth was made up to a sullen
expression, and when her brother was shown
to her she did not hold out her arms to him
nor vouchsafe a kiss.

The Queen looked at her wistfully, asking—

'Is he not like the King?'

'Humph!' returned Princess Anne, 'I
see no likeness to any living soul of our
family.'

'Nay, but see his little nails,' said the
Queen, spreading the tiny hand over her
finger. 'See how like your father's they are
framed! My treasure, you can clasp me!'

'My brother, Edgar! He was the beauty,'
said the Princess. '*He* was exactly like my

father; but there's no judging of anything so puny as this!'

'He was very suffering last week, the poor little angel,' said the mother sadly; 'but they say this water-gruel is very nourishing, and not so heavy as milk.'

'It does not look as if it agreed with him,' said the Princess. 'Poor little mammet! Did I hear that you had the little Woodford here? Is that you, girl?'

Anne courtesied herself forward.

'Ay, I remember you. I never forget a face, and you have grown up fair enough. Where's your mother?'

'I lost her last February, so please your Royal Highness.'

'Oh! She was a good woman. Why did she not send you to me? Well, well! Come to my toilet to-morrow.'

So Princess Anne swept away in her rich blue brocade. Her behest was obeyed, of course, though it was evidently displeasing to the nursery authorities, and Lady Strickland gave a warning to be discreet and to avoid gossip with the Cockpit folks.

Anne could not but be excited. Perhaps

the Princess would ask for her, and take her into the number of her own attendants, where she would no longer be in a Romish household, and would certainly be in a higher position. Why, she remembered that very Lady Churchill as Sarah Jennings in no better a position than she could justly aspire to. Her coming to Court would thus be truly justified.

The Princess sat in a silken wrapper, called a night-gown, in her chamber, which had a richly curtained bed in the alcove, and a toilet-table with a splendid Venetian mirror, and a good deal of silver sparkling on it, while a strange mixture of perfumes came from the various boxes and bottles. Ladies and tirewomen stood in attendance; a little black boy in a turban and gold-embroidered dress held a salver with her chocolate cup; a cockatoo soliloquised in low whispers in the window; a monkey was chained to a pole at a safe distance from him; a French friseur was manipulating the Princess's profuse brown hair with his tongs; and a needy-looking, pale thin man, in a semi-clerical suit, was half-reading, half-declaiming a poem, in which 'Fair Anna' seemed mixed up with

Juno, Ceres, and other classical folk, but to which she was evidently paying very little attention.

'Ah! there you are, little one. Thank you, Master—what's name; that is enough. 'Tis a fine poem, but I never can remember which is which of all your gods and goddesses. Oh yes, I accept the dedication. Give him a couple of guineas, Ellis; it will serve him for board and lodging for a fortnight, poor wretch!' Then, after giving a smooth, well-shaped white hand to be kissed, and inviting her visitor to a cushion at her feet, she began a long series of questions, kindly ones at first, though of the minute gossiping kind, and extending to the Archfields, for poor young Madam had been of the rank about which royalty knew everything in those days. The inquiries were extremely minute, and the comments what from any one else, Anne would have thought vulgar, especially in the presence of the hairdresser, but her namesake observed her blush and hesitation, and said, 'Oh, never mind a creature like that. He is French, besides, and does not understand a word we say.'

Anne, looking over the Princess's head, feared that she saw a twinkle in the man's eye, and could only look down and try to ignore him through the catechism that ensued, on when she came to Whitehall, on the Prince of Wales's health, the management of him, and all the circumstances connected with his birth.

Very glad was Anne that she knew nothing, and had not picked up any information as to what had happened before she came to the palace. As to the present, Lady Strickland's warning and her own sense of honour kept her reticent to a degree that evidently vexed the Princess, for she dropped her caressing manner, and sent her away with a not very kind, 'You may go now; you will be turning Papist next, and what would your poor mother say?'

And as Anne departed in backward fashion she heard Lady Churchill say, 'You will make nothing of her. She is sharper than she affects, and a proud minx! I see it in her carriage.'

The visit had only dashed a few hopes and done her harm with her immediate surroundings, who always disliked and distrusted intercourse with the other establishment.

However, in another day the nursery was moved to Richmond. This was a welcome move to Anne, who had spent her early childhood near enough to be sometimes taken thither, and to know the Park well, so that there was a home feeling in the sight of the outline of the trees and the scenery of the neighbourhood. The Queen intended going to Bath, so that the establishment was only that of the Prince, and the life was much quieter on the whole; but there was no gratifying any yearning for country walks, for it was not safe nor perhaps decorous for one young woman to be out alone in a park open to the public and haunted by soldiers from Hounslow—nor could either of her fellow-rockers understand her preference for a secluded path through the woods. Miss Dunord never went out at all, except on duty, when the Prince was carried along the walks in the garden, and the other two infinitely preferred the open spaces, where tables were set under the horse-chestnut trees for parties who boated down from London to eat curds and whey, sometimes bringing a fiddler so as to dance under the trees.

Jane Humphreys especially was always looking out for acquaintances, and once, with a cry of joy, a stout, homely-looking young woman started up, exclaiming, 'Sister Jane!' and flew into her arms. Upon which Miss Woodford was introduced to 'My sister Coles' and her husband, and had to sit down under a tree and share the festivities, while there was an overflow of inquiries and intelligence, domestic and otherwise. Certainly these were persons whom she would not have treated as equals at home.

Besides, it was all very well to hear of the good old grandmother's rheumatics, and of little Tommy's teething, and even to see Jane hang her head and be teased about remembering Mr. Hopkins; nor was it wonderful to hear lamentations over the extreme dulness of the life where one never saw a creature to speak to who was not as old as the hills; but when it came to inquiries as minute as the Princess's about the Prince of Wales, Anne thought the full details lavishly poured out scarcely consistent with loyalty to their oaths of service and Lady Strickland's warning, and she told Jane so.

She was answered, 'Oh la! what harm can it do? You are such a proud peat! Grand-dame and sister like to know all about His Royal Highness.'

This was true; but Anne was far more uncomfortable two or three days later. The Prince was ailing, so much so that Lady Powys had sent an express for the Queen, who had not yet started for Bath, when Anne and Jane, being relieved from duty by the other pair, went out for a stroll.

'Oh la!' presently exclaimed Jane, 'if that is not Colonel Sands, the Princess's equerry. I do declare he is coming to speak to us, though he is one of the Cockpit folks.'

He was a very fine gentleman indeed, all scarlet and gold, and no wonder Jane was flattered and startled, so that she jerked her fan violently up and down as he accosted her with a wave of his cocked hat, saying that he was rejoiced to meet these two fair ladies, having been sent by the Princess of Denmark to inquire for the health of the Prince. She was very anxious to know more than could be learnt by formal inquiry, he said, and he was happy to have met the young gentlewomen who could gratify him.

The term 'gentlewoman' highly flattered Miss Humphreys, who blushed and bridled, and exclaimed, 'Oh la, sir!' but Anne thought it needful to say gravely—

'We are in trust, sir, and have no right to speak of what passes within the royal household.'

'Madam, I admire your discretion, but to the—(a-hem)—sister of the—(a-hem)—Prince of Wales it is surely uncalled for.'

'Miss Woodford is so precise,' said Jane Humphreys, with a giggle; 'I do not know what harm can come of saying that His Royal Highness peaks and pines just as he did before.'

'He is none the better for country air then?'

'Oh no! except that he cries louder. Such a time as we had last night! Mrs. Royer never slept a wink all the time I was there, but walked about with him all night. You had the best of it, Miss Woodford.'

'He slept while I was there,' said Anne

briefly, not thinking it needful to state that the tired nurse had handed the child over to her, and that he had fallen asleep in her arms. She tried to put an end to the conversation by going indoors, but she was vexed to find that, instead of following her closely, Miss Humphreys was still lingering with the equerry.

Anne found the household in commotion. Pauline met her, weeping bitterly, and saying the Prince had had a fit, and all hope was over, and in the rockers' room she found Hester Bridgeman exclaiming that her occupation was gone. Water-gruel, she had no doubt, had been the death of the Prince. The Queen was come, and wellnigh distracted. She had sent out in quest of a wet-nurse, but it was too late; he was going the way of all Her Majesty's children.

Going down again together the two girls presently had to stand aside as the poor Queen, seeing and hearing nothing, came towards her own room with her handkerchief over her face. They pressed each other's hands awe-stricken, and went on to the nursery. There Mrs. Labadie was kneeling over the cradle, her hood hanging over her face, crying bitterly over the poor little child, who had a blue look about his face, and seemed at the last gasp, his features contorted by a convulsion.

At that moment Jane Humphreys was seen gently opening the door and letting in Colonel Sands, who moved as quietly as possible, to give a furtive look at the dying child. His researches were cut short, however. Lady Strickland, usually the gentlest of women, darted out and demanded what he was doing in her nursery.

He attempted to stammer some excuse about Princess Anne, but Lady Strickland only answered by standing pointing to the door, and he was forced to retreat in a very undignified fashion.

'Who brought him?' she demanded, when the door was shut. 'Those Cockpit folk are not to come prying here, hap what may!'

Miss Humphreys had sped away for fear of questions being asked, and attention was diverted by Mrs. Royer arriving with a stout, healthy-looking young woman in a thick home-spun cloth petticoat, no stockings, and old shoes, but with a clean white cap on her head—a tilemaker's wife who had been captured in the village.

No sooner was the suffering, half-starved child delivered over to her than he became serene and contented. The water-gruel regime was over, and he began to thrive from that time. Even when later in the afternoon the King himself brought in Colonel Sands, whom in the joy of his heart he had asked to dine with him, the babe lay tranquilly on the cradle, waving his little hands and looking happy.

The intrusion seemed to have been forgotten, but that afternoon Anne, who had been sent on a message to one of the Queen's ladies, more than suspected that she saw Jane in a deep recess of a window in confabulation with the Colonel. And when they were alone at bed-time the girl said—

'Is it not droll? The Colonel cannot believe that 'tis the same child. He has been joking and teasing me to declare that we have a dead Prince hidden somewhere, and that the King showed him the brick-bat woman's child.'

'How can you prattle in that mischievous way—after what Lady Strickland said, too? You do not know what harm you may do!'

'Oh lack, it was all a jest!'

'I am not so sure that it was.'

'But you will not tell of me, dear friend, you will not. I never saw Lady Strickland like that; I did not know she could be in such a rage.'

'No wonder, when a fellow like that came peeping and prying like a raven to see whether the poor babe was still breathing,' cried Anne indignantly. 'How could you bring him in?'

'Fellow indeed! Why he is a colonel in the Life-guards, and the Princess's equerry; and who has a right to know about the child if not his own sister—or half-sister?'

'She is not a very loving sister,' replied Anne. 'You know well, Jane, how many would not be sorry to make out that it is as that man would fain have you say.'

'Well, I told him it was no such thing, and laughed the very notion to scorn.'

'It were better not to talk with him at all.'

'But you will not speak of it. If I were

turned away my father would beat me. Nay, I know not what he might not do to me. You will not tell, dear darling Portia, and I will love you for ever.'

'I have no call to tell,' said Anne coldly, but she was disgusted and weary, and moreover not at all sure that she, as the other Protestant rocker, and having been in the Park on that same day, was not credited with some of the mischievous gossip that had passed.

'There, Portia, that is what you get by walking with that stupid Humphreys,' said Oriana. 'She knows no better than to blab to any one who will be at the trouble to seem sweet upon her, though she may get nothing by it.'

'Would it be better if she did?' asked Anne.

'Oh, well, we must all look out for ourselves, and I am sure there is no knowing what may come next. But I hear we are to move to Windsor as soon as the child is strong enough, so as to be farther out of reach of the Cockpit tongues.'

This proved to be true, but the Prince

and his suite were not lodged in the Castle itself, a house in the cloisters being thought more suitable, and here the Queen visited her child daily, for since that last alarm she could not bear to be long absent from him. Such emissaries as Colonel Sands did not again appear, but after that precedent Lady Strickland had become much more unwilling to allow any of those under her authority to go out into any public place, and the rockers seldom got any exercise except as swelling the Prince's train when he was carried out to take the air.

Anne looked with longing eyes at the Park, but a ramble there was a forbidden pleasure. She could not always even obtain leave to attend St. George's Chapel ; the wish was treated as a sort of weakness, or folly, and she was always the person selected to stay at home when any religious ceremony called away the rest of the establishment.

As the King's god-daughter it was impressed on her that she ought to conform to his Church, and one of the many priests about the Court was appointed to instruct her. In the dearth of all intellectual intercourse, and the absolute deficiency of books, she could not but become deeply interested in the arguments. Her uncle had forearmed her with instruction, and she wrote to him on any difficulty which arose, and this became the chief occupation of her mind, distracting her thoughts from the one great cloud that hung over her memory. Indeed one of the foremost bulwarks her feelings erected to fortify her conscience against the temptations around, was the knowledge that she would have, though of course under seal of confession, to relate that terrible story to a priest.

Hester Bridgeman could not imagine how her Portia could endure to hear the old English Prayer-book droned out. For her part, she liked one thing or the other, either a rousing Nonconformist sermon in a meeting-house or a splendid Mass.

'But, after all,' as Anne overheard her observing to Miss Dunord, 'it may be all the better for us. What with her breeding and her foreign tongues, she would be sure to be set over our heads as under-governess, or the like, if she were not such an obstinate heretic, and keeping that stupid Humphreys so. We could have converted her long ago, if it were not for that Woodford and for her City grand-dame! Portia is the King's godchild, too, so it is just as well that she does not see what is for her own advantage.'

'I do not care for promotion. I only want to save my own soul and hers,' said Pauline. 'I wish she would come over to the true Church, for I could love her.'

And certainly Pauline Dunord's gentle devotional example, and her perfect rest and peace in the practice of her religion, were strong influences with Anne. She was waiting till circumstances should make it possible to her to enter a convent, and in the meantime she lived a strictly devout life, abstracted as far as duty and kindness permitted from the little cabals and gossipry around.

Anne could not help feeling that the girl was as nearly a saint as any one she had ever seen—far beyond herself in goodness. Moreover, the Queen inspired strong affection. Mary Beatrice was not only a very beautiful person, full of the grace and dignity of the House of Este, but she was deeply religious, good and gentle, kindly and gracious to all who approached her, and devoted to her husband and child. A word or look from her was always a delight, and Anne, by her knowledge of Italian, was able sometimes to obtain a smiling word or remark.

The little Prince, after those first miserable weeks of his life, had begun to thrive, and by and by manifested a decided preference not only for his beautiful mother, but for the fresh face, bright smile, and shining brown eyes of Miss Woodford. She could almost always, with nods and becks, avert a passion of roaring, which sometimes went beyond the powers of even his foster-mother, the tiler's wife. The Queen watched with delight when he laughed and flourished his arms in response, and the King was summoned to see the performance, which he requited by taking out a fat gold watch set with pearls, and presenting it to Anne, as his grave gloomy face lighted up with a smile.

'Are you yet one of us?' he asked, as she received his gift on her knee.

'No, sir, I cannot——'

'That must be amended. You have read his late Majesty's paper?'

'I have, sir.'

'And seen Father Giverlai?'

'Yes, please your Majesty.'

'And still you are not convinced. That must not be. I would gladly consider and promote you, but I can only have true Catholics around my son. I shall desire Father Crump to see you.'

CHAPTER XVIII

HALLOWMAS EVE

> 'This more strange
> Than such a murder is.' *Macbeth.*

'*Bambino mio, bambino mio,*' wailed Mary Beatrice, as she pressed her child to her bosom, and murmured to him in her native tongue. 'And did they say he was not his mother's son, his poor mother, whose dearest treasure he is! *Oimè, crudeli, crudelissimi!* Even his sisters hate him and will not own him, the little jewel of his mother's heart!'

Anne, waiting in the window, was grieved to have overheard the words which the poor Queen had poured out, evidently thinking no one near could understand her.

That evening there were orders to prepare for a journey to Whitehall the next morning.

'And,' said Hester Bridgeman, 'I can tell

you why, in all confidence, but I have it from a sure hand. The Prince of Orange is collecting a fleet and army to come and inquire into certain matters, especially into the birth of a certain young gentleman we wot of.'

'How can he have the insolence?' cried Anne.

''Tis no great wonder, considering the vipers in the Cockpit,' said Hester.

'But what will they do to us?' asked Jane Humphreys in terror.

'Nothing to you, my dear, nor to Portia; you are good Protestants,' said Hester with a sneer.

'Mrs. Royer told me it was for the christening,' said Jane, 'and then we shall all have new suits. I am glad we are going back to town. It cannot be so mortal dull as 'tis here, with all the leaves falling—enough to give one the vapours.'

There were auguries on either hand in the palace that if the Prince came it would be only another Monmouth affair, and this made Anne shrink, for she had partaken of the grief and indignation of Winchester at the cruel execution of Lady Lisle, and had heard rumours enough of the progress of the Assize to make her start in horror when called to watch the red-faced Lord Chancellor Jeffreys getting out of his coach.

It really seemed for the time as if the royal household were confident in this impression, though as soon as they were again settled in Whitehall there was a very close examination of the witnesses of the Prince's birth, and a report printed of their evidence, enough it might be thought to satisfy any one; but Jane Humphreys, who went to spend a day at the Golden Lamb, her father's warehouse, reported that people only laughed at it.

Anne's spirit burned at the injustice, and warmed the more towards the Queen and little Prince, whose pretty responses to her caresses could not but win her love. Moreover, Pauline's example continued to attract her, and Father Crump was a better controversialist, or perhaps a better judge of character, than Père Giverlai, and took her on sides where she was more vulnerable, so as to make her begin to feel unsettled, and wonder whether she were not making a vain sacrifice, and holding out after all against the better way.

The sense of the possible gain, and disgust at the shallow conversions of some around her, helped to keep her back. She could not help observing that while Pauline persuaded, Hester had ceased to persuade, and seemed rather willing to hinder her. Just before the State christening, or rather admission into the Church, Lady Powys, in the name of the King and Queen, offered her the post of sub-governess, which really would mean for the present chief playfellow to the little Prince, and would place her on an entirely different platform of society from the comparatively menial one she occupied, but of course on the condition of conformity to Rome.

To be above the familiarity of Jane and Hester was no small temptation, but still she hesitated.

'Madam, I thank you, I thank their Majesties,' she said, 'but I cannot do it thus.'

'I see what you mean, Miss Woodford,' said Lady Powys, who was a truly noble woman. 'Your motives must be above suspicion even to yourself. I respect you, and would not have made you the offer except by express command, but I still trust that when your disinterestedness is above suspicion you will still join us.'

It was sore mortification when Hester Bridgeman was preferred to the office, for which she was far less fitted, being no favourite with the babe, and being essentially vulgar in tastes and habits, and knowing no language save her own, and that ungrammatically and with an accent which no one could wish the Prince to acquire. Yet there she was, promoted to the higher grade of the establishment and at the christening, standing in the front ranks, while Miss Woodford was left far in the rear among the servants.

A report of the Dutch fleet having been destroyed by a storm had restored the spirits of the Court; and in the nursery very little was known of the feelings of the kingdom at large. Dr. Woodford did not venture on writing freely to his niece, lest he should compromise her, and she only vaguely detected that he was uneasy.

So came All Saints' Day Eve, when there was to be a special service late in the evening at the Romanised Chapel Royal at St. James's, with a sermon by a distinguished Dominican, to which all the elder and graver members of the household were eager to go. And there was another very different attraction at the Cockpit, where good-natured Princess Anne had given permission for a supper, to be followed by burning of nuts and all the divinations proper to Hallowmas Eve, to which were invited all the subordinates of the Whitehall establishment who could be spared.

Pauline Dunord was as eager for the sermon as Jane Humphreys was for the supper, and Hester Bridgeman was in an odd mood of uncertainty, evidently longing after the sports, but not daring to show that she did so, and trying to show great desire to hear the holy man preach, together with a polite profession of self-denial in giving up her place in case there should not be room for all. However, as it appeared that even the two chief nurses meant to combine sermon and the latter end of the supper, she was at ease. The foster-mother and one of the

Protestant rockers were supposed to be enough to watch over the Prince, but the former, who had been much petted and spoilt since she had been at the palace, and was a young creature, untrained and wilful, cried so much at the idea of missing the merrymaking, that as it was reckoned important to keep her in good humour and good spirits, Mrs. Labadie decided on winking at her absence from the nursery, since Miss Woodford was quite competent to the charge for the short time that both the church-goers and the supper-goers would all be absent together.

'But are you not afraid to stay alone?' asked Mrs. Labadie, with a little compunction.

'What is there to be afraid of?' asked Anne. 'There are the sentinels at the foot of the stairs, and what should reach us here?'

'I would not be alone here,' said more than one voice. 'Nor I!'—'Nor I!'

'And on this night of all others!' said Hester.

'But why?'

'They say he walks!' whispered Jane in a voice of awe.

'Who walks?'

'The old King?' asked Hester.

'No; the last King,' said Jane.

'No, no; it was Oliver Cromwell—old Noll himself!' put in another voice.

'I tell you, no such thing,' said Jane. 'It was the last King. I heard it from them that saw it, at least the lady's cousin. 'Twas in the long gallery, in a suit of plain black velvet, with white muslin ruffles and cravat quilled very neat. Why do you laugh, Miss Woodford?'

This was too much for Anne, who managed to say, 'Who was his laundress?'

'I tell you I heard it from them that told no lies. The gentleman could swear to it. He took a candle to him, and there was nought but the wainscot behind. Think of that.'

'And that we should be living here!' said another voice.

'I never venture about the big draughty place alone at night,' said the laundress.

'No! nor I would not for twenty princes,' added the sempstress.

'Nay, I have heard steps,' said Mrs.

Royer, 'and wailing—wailing. No wonder after all that has happened here. Oh yes, steps as of the guard being turned out!'

'That is like our Squire's manor-house, where——'

Every one contributed a story, and only the announcement of Her Majesty's approach put an end to these reminiscences.

Anne held to her purpose. She had looked forward to this time of solitude, for she wanted leisure to consider the situation, and fairly to revolve the pleas by which Father Crump had shaken her, more in feeling than in her reason, and made her question whether her allegiance to her mother and uncle, and her disgust at interested conversions, were not making her turn aside from what might be the only true Church, the Mother of Saints, and therewith perversely give up earthly advancement. But oh! how to write to her uncle.

The very intention made her imagination and memory too powerful for the consideration of controversy. She went back first to a merry Hallowmas Eve long ago, among the Archfield party and other Winchester friends, and how the nuts had bounced in a manner which made the young ones shout in ecstasy of glee, but seemed to displease some of the elders, and had afterwards been the occasion of her being told that it was all folly, and therewith informed of Charles Archfield's contract to poor little Alice Fitzhubert. Then came other scenes. All the various ghostly tales she had heard, and as she sat with her knitting in the shaded room with no sound but the soft breathing of her little charge in his cradle, no light save from a shaded lamp and the fire on the hearth, strange thoughts and dreams floated over her; she started at mysterious cracks in the wainscotting from time to time, and beheld in the dark corners of the great room forms that seemed grotesque and phantom-like till she went up to them and resolved them into familiar bits of furniture or gowns and caps of Mrs. Labadie. She repeated half aloud numerous Psalms and bits of poetry, but in the midst would come some disturbing noise, a step or a shout from the street, though the chamber being at the back of the house looking into the Park few of such sounds penetrated thither. She began to think of King Charles's last walk from St. James's to Whitehall, and of the fatal window of the Banqueting-hall which had been pointed out to her, and then her thoughts flew back again to that vault in the castle yard, and she saw only too vividly in memory that open vault, veiled partly by nettles and mulleins, which was the unblest, unknown grave of the old playfellow who had so loved her mother and herself. Perhaps she had hitherto more dwelt on and pitied the living than the dead, as one whom fears and prayers still concerned, but now as she thought of the lively sprite-like being who had professed such affection for her, and for whom her mother had felt so much, and recollected him so soon and suddenly cut down and consigned to that dreary darkness, the strange yearning spirit dismissed to the unknown world, instead of her old terror and repulsion, a great tenderness and compunction came over her, and she longed to join those who would in two days more be keeping All Souls' Day in intercessions for their departed, so as to atone for her past dislike; and there was that sort of feeling about her which can only be described by the word 'eerie.' To relieve it Anne walked to the window and undid a small wicket in the shutter, so as to look out into the quiet moonlight park where the trees cast their long shadows on the silvery grass, and there was a great calm that seemed to reach her heart and spirits.

Suddenly, across the sward towards the palace there came the slight, impish, almost one-sided figure, with the peculiar walk, swift though suggestive of a limp, the elfish set of the plume, the foreign adjustment of short cloak. Anne gazed with wide-stretched eyes and beating heart, trying to rally her senses and believe it fancy, when the figure crossed into a broad streak of light cast by the lamp over the door, the face was upturned for a moment. It was deadly pale, and the features were beyond all doubt Peregrine Oakshott's.

She sprang back from the window, dropped on her knees, with her face hidden in her hands, and was hardly conscious till sounds of the others returning made her rally her powers so as to prevent all inquiries or surmises. It was Mrs. Labadie and Pauline Dunord, the former to see that all was well with the Prince before repairing to the Cockpit.

'How pale you are!' she exclaimed. 'Have you seen anything?'

'I— It may be nothing. He is dead!' stammered Anne.

'Oh then, 'tis naught but a maid's fancies,' said the nurse good-humouredly. 'Miss Dunord is in no mind for the sports, so she will stay with His Highness, and you had best come with me and drive the cobwebs out of your brain.'

'Indeed, I thank you, ma'am, but I could not,' said Anne.

'You had best, I tell you, shake these megrims out of your brain,' said Mrs. Labadie; but she was in too great haste not to lose her share of the amusements to argue the point, and the two young women were left together. Pauline was in a somewhat exalted state, full of the sermon on the connection of the Church with the invisible world.

'You have seen one of your poor dead,' she said. 'Oh, may it not be that he came to implore you to have pity, and join the Church, where you could intercede and offer the Holy Sacrifice for him?'

Anne started. This seemed to chime in with proclivities of poor Peregrine's own, and when she thought of his corpse in that unhallowed vault, it seemed to her as if he must be calling on her to take measures for his rest, both of body and of spirit. Yet something seemed to seal her tongue. She could not open her lips on what she had seen, and while Pauline talked on, repeating the sermon which had so deeply touched her feelings, Anne heard without listening to aught besides her own perturbations, mentally debating whether she could endure to reveal the story to Father Crump, if she confessed to him, or whether she should write to her uncle; and she even began to compose the letter in her own mind, with the terrible revelation that must commence it, but every moment the idea became more formidable. How transfer her own heavy burthen to her uncle, who might feel bound to take steps that would cut young Archfield off from parents, sister, child, and home. Or supposing Dr. Woodford disbelieved the apparition of to-night, the whole would be discredited in his eyes, and he might suppose the summer morning's duel as much a delusion of her fancy as the autumn evening's phantom; and what evidence had she to adduce save Charles's despair, Peregrine's absence, and what there might be in the vault?

Yet if all that Father Crump and Pauline said was true, that dear uncle might be under a fatal delusion, and it might be the best hope for herself—nay, even for that poor restless spirit—to separate herself from them. Here was Pauline talking of the blessedness of being able to offer prayers on 'All Souls' Day' for all those of whose ultimate salvation there were fears, or who might be in a state of suffering. It even startled her as she thought of her mother, whom she always gave thanks for as one departed in faith and fear. Would Father Crump speak of her as one in a state of inevitable ignorance to be expiated in the invisible world? It shocked the daughter as almost profane. Yet if it were true, and prayers and masses could aid her?

Altogether Anne was in a mood on which the voices broke strangely returning from the supper full of news. Jane Humphreys was voluble on her various experiments. The nuts had burnt quietly together, and that was propitious to the Life-guardsman, Mr. Shaw, who had shared hers; but on the other hand, the apple-paring thrown over her shoulder had formed a P, and he whom she had seen in the vista of looking-glasses had a gold chain but neither a uniform nor a P in his name, and Mrs. Buss declared that it meant that she should be three times married, and the last would be an Alderman, if not Lord Mayor; and Mrs. Royer was joking Miss Bridgeman on the I of her apple-paring, which could stand for nothing but a certain Incle among 'the Cockpit folk,' who was her special detestation.

Princess Anne and her husband had come down to see the nuts flying, and had laughed enough to split their sides, till Lord Cornbury came in and whispered something to Prince George, who said, '*Est il possible?*' and spoke to the Princess, and they all went away together. Yes, and the Bishop of Bath and Wells, who had been laughing before looked very grave, and went with them.

'Oh!' exclaimed Anne, 'is the Bishop of Bath and Wells here?'

'Yes, in spite of his disgrace. I hear he is to preach in your Protestant chapel tomorrow.'

Anne had brought a letter of introduction from her uncle in case she should have any opportunity of seeing his old fellow canon, who had often been kind to her when she was a little girl at Winchester. She was in many minds of hope and fear as to the meeting him or speaking to him, under the consciousness of the possible defection from his Church, and the doubt and dread whether to confide her secret and consult him. However, the extreme improbability of her being able to do so made the yearning for the sight of a Winchester face predominate, and her vigil of the night past made the nursery authorities concede that she had fairly earned her turn to go to church in the forenoon, since she was obstinate enough to want to run after an old heretic so-called Bishop who had so pragmatically withstood His Majesty. Jane Humphreys went too, for though she was not fond of week-day services, any escape from the nursery was welcome, and there was a chance of seeing Lady Churchill's new mantle.

In this she was disappointed, for none of the grandees were present, indeed it was whispered as the two girls made their way to the chapel, that there was great excitement over the Declaration of the Prince of Orange, which had arrived last night, that he had been invited by the lords spiritual and temporal to take up the cause of the liberties of England, and inquire into the evidence of the birth of the Prince of Wales.

People shrugged their shoulders, but looked volumes, though it was no time nor place for saying more; and when in the chapel, that countenance of Bishop Ken, so beautiful in outward form, so expressive of strength, sweetness, and devotion, brought back such a flood of old associations to Anne, that it was enough to change the whole current of her thoughts and make her her own mother's child again, even before he opened his mouth. She caught his sweet voice in the Psalms, and closing her eyes seemed to be in the Cathedral once more among those mighty columns and arches; and when he began his sermon, on the text, 'Let the Saints be joyful with glory, let them rejoice in their beds,' she found the Communion of Saints in Paradise and on earth knit together in one fellowship as truly and preciously brought home to her as ever it had been to Pauline, and moreover when she thought of her mother, 'the lurid mist' was dispelled which had so haunted her the night before.

The longing to speak to him awoke; and as he was quitting the chapel in full procession his kindly eye lit upon her with a look of recognition; and before she had moved from her place, one of the attendant clergy came back by his desire to conduct her to him.

He held out his hand as she courtesied low.

'Mistress Woodford,' he said, 'my old friend's niece! He wrote to me of you, but I have had no opportunity of seeing you before.'

'Oh, my Lord! I was so much longing to see and speak with you.'

'I am lodging at Lambeth,' said the Bishop, 'and it is too far to take you with me thither, but perhaps my good brother here,' turning to the chaplain, 'can help us to a room where we can be private.'

This was done; the chaplain's parlour at the Cockpit was placed at their disposal, and there a few kind words from Bishop Ken led to the unburthening of her heavy heart. Of Ken's replies to the controversial difficulties there is no need to tell. Indeed, ambition was far more her temptation than any real difficulties as to doctrine. Her dissatisfaction at being unable to answer the questions raised by Father Crump was exaggerated as the excuse and cover to herself of her craving for escape from her present subordinate post; and this the Bishop soon saw, and tenderly but firmly drew her to own both this and to confess the ambitious spirit which had led her into this scene of temptation. 'It was true indeed,' he said, 'that trial by our own error is hardest to encounter, but you have repented, and by God's grace, my child, I trust you will be enabled to steer your course aright through the trials of loyalty to our God and to our King that are coming upon us all. Ever remember God and the plain duty first, His anointed next. Is there more that you would like to tell me? for you still bear a troubled look, and I have full time.'

Then Anne told him all the strange adventure of Portchester Castle, and even of the apparition of the night before. That gentleness and sympathy seemed to draw out all that was in her heart, and to her surprise, he did not treat the story of that figure as necessarily a delusion. He had known and heard too much of spiritual manifestations to the outward senses to declare that such things could not be.

What she had seen might be explained by one of four hypotheses. It was either a phantom of her brain, and her being fully awake, although recently dwelling on the recollection, rendered that idea less probable, or the young man had not been killed, and she had seen him in *propriâ personâ*.

She had Charles Archfield's word that the death was certain. He had never been heard of again, and if alive, the walk before Whitehall was the last place where he would be. As to mistaking any one else for him, the Bishop remembered enough of the queer changeling elf to agree with her that it was not a very probable contingency. And if it were indeed a spirit, why should it visit her? There had been one good effect certainly in the revival of home thoughts and turning her mind from the allurements of favour, but that did not seem to account for the spirit seeking her out.

Was it, Anne faltered, a sign that she ought to confess all, for the sake of procuring Christian burial for him. Yet how should she, when she had promised silence to young Archfield? True, it was for his wife's sake, and she was dead; but there were the rest of his family and himself to be considered. What should she do?

The Bishop thought a little while, then said that he did not believe that she ought to speak without Mr. Archfield's consent, unless she saw any one else brought into danger by her silence. If it ever became possible, he thought, that she should ascertain whether the body were in the vault, and if so, it might be possible to procure burial for it, perhaps without identification, or at any rate without making known what could only cause hostility and distress between the two families, unless the young man himself on his return should make the confession. This the Bishop evidently considered the sounder, though the harder course, but he held that Anne had no right to take the initiative. She could only wait, and bear her load alone; but the extreme kindness and compassion with which he talked to her soothed and comforted her so much that she felt infinitely relieved and strengthened when he dismissed her with his blessing, and far happier and more at peace than she had been since that terrible summer morning, though greatly humbled, and taught to repent of her aspirations after earthly greatness, and to accept her present condition as a just retribution, and a trial of constancy.

END OF VOL. I.

Printed by R. & R. CLARK, *Edinburgh.*

MESSRS. MACMILLAN & CO.'S PUBLICATIONS.

CHEAP EDITION OF THE NOVELS AND TALES

OF

CHARLOTTE M. YONGE.

A complete uniform and Cheaper Edition in Twenty-Eight Volumes, with all the original Illustrations. Crown 8vo. 3s. 6d. each. To be published fortnightly as follows :—

The Heir of Redclyffe.	*Ready.*	The Chaplet of Pearls.	*Ready.*
Heartsease.	,,	Lady Hester, and the Danvers Papers.	
Hopes and Fears.	,,		,,
Dynevor Terrace.	,,	Magnum Bonum.	,,
The Daisy Chain.	,,	Love and Life.	,,
The Trial: More Links of the Daisy Chain.	,,	Unknown to History.	,,
		Stray Pearls.	,,
Pillars of the House. Vol. I.	,,	The Armourer's 'Prentices.	,,
Pillars of the House. Vol. II.	,,	The Two Sides of the Shield.	,,
The Young Stepmother.	,,	Nuttie's Father.	,,
Clever Woman of the Family.	,,	Scenes and Characters.	
The Three Brides.	,,	Chantry House.	*Oct.* 1.
My Young Alcides.	,,	A Modern Telemachus.	,, 15.
The Caged Lion.	,,	Eyewords.	*Nov.* 1.
The Dove in the Eagle's Nest.	,,	Beechcroft at Rockstone.	,, 15.

CHEAP EDITION OF SELECTED WORKS

OF

CHARLES KINGSLEY.

In Eighteen Volumes. Crown 8vo. 3s. 6d. each.

Westward Ho!	*Ready.*	Plays and Puritans, and other Historical Essays.	*Oct.* 1889.
Hypatia.	,,		
Yeast.	,,	The Roman and the Teuton.	*Nov.* 1889.
Alton Locke.	,,		
Two Years Ago.	,,	Sanitary and Social Lectures and Essays.	*Dec.* 1889.
Hereward the Wake.	,,		
Poems.	,,	Historical Lectures and Essays.	*Jan.* 1890.
The Heroes.	,,		
The Water-Babies.	,,	Scientific Lectures and Essays.	*Feb.* 1890.
Madam How and Lady Why.	,,		
At Last.	,,	Literary and General Lectures.	*March* 1890.
Prose Idylls.	,,		

MACMILLAN AND CO., LONDON.

WORKS BY CHARLOTTE M. YONGE.

Beechcroft at Rockstone. Two Vols. Crown 8vo. 12s.

A Reputed Changeling. Two Vols. Crown 8vo. 12s.

Byewords: A Collection of Tales New and Old. Crown 8vo. 6s.

The Prince and the Page: A tale of the Last Crusade. Illustrated. New Edition. Globe 8vo. 4s. 6d.

Little Lucy's Wonderful Globe. With Twenty-four Illustrations by FROLICH. New Edition. Globe 8vo. 4s. 6d.

A Book of Golden Deeds. 18mo. 4s. 6d. Globe Readings. Edition for Schools. Globe 8vo. 2s. Cheap Edition. 1s. Third Edition. Illustrated. Crown 8vo. 6s.

The Story of the Christians and the Moors in Spain. With a Vignette by HOLMAN HUNT. 18mo. 4s. 6d.

P's and Q's; or, The Question of Putting Upon. With Illustrations by C. O. MURRAY. Third Edition. Globe 8vo. Cloth gilt. 4s. 6d.

The Lances of Lynwood. With Illustrations. New Edition. Globe 8vo. 4s. 6d.

The Little Duke. New Edition. Globe 8vo. 4s. 6d.

A Storehouse of Stories. Edited by. Two Vols. Each 2s. 6d.

A Book of Worthies. Gathered from the Old Histories and written Anew. 18mo. Cloth extra. 4s. 6d.

The Population of an Old Pear Tree; or, Stories of Insect Life. From the French of E. VAN BRUYSSEL. With numerous Illustrations by BECKER. New Edition. Globe 8vo. 2s. 6d.

Cameos from English History. Vol. I. From Rollo to Edward II. Extra fcap. 8vo. 5s. Vol. II. The Wars in France. 5s. Vol. III. The Wars of the Roses. 5s. Vol. IV. Reformation Times. 5s. Vol. V. England and Spain. 5s. Vol. VI. Forty Years of Stuart Rule, 1603-1643. 5s. Vol. VII. The Rebellion and Restoration, 1642-1678. 5s.

A Parallel History of France and England, consisting of Outlines and Dates. Oblong 4to. 3s. 6d.

Scripture Readings for Schools and Families. Globe 8vo. 1s. 6d. each. Also with Comments, 3s. 6d. each. First Series: Genesis to Deuteronomy. Second Series: Joshua to Solomon. Third Series: Kings and Prophets. Fourth Series: The Gospel Times. Fifth Series: Apostolic Times.

History of Christian Names. New and Revised Edition. Crown 8vo. 7s. 6d.

The Life of John Coleridge Patteson, Missionary Bishop. New Edition. Two Vols. Crown 8vo. 12s.

The Pupils of St. John. Illustrated. Crown 8vo. 6s.

Pioneers and Founders; or, Recent Workers in the Mission Field. Crown 8vo. 6s.

The Herb of the Field: Reprinted from "Chapters on Flowers" in *The Magazine for the Young*. A New Edition, Revised and Corrected. Crown 8vo. 5s.

The Victorian Half Century. Crown 8vo, Paper Covers. 1s. Limp cloth, 1s. 6d.

MACMILLAN AND CO., LONDON.

MACMILLAN'S TWO SHILLING NOVELS.

Price 2s. each Volume. Globe 8vo.

BY THE AUTHOR OF "JOHN HALIFAX, GENTLEMAN."

TWO MARRIAGES.
OLIVE.
AGATHA'S HUSBAND.
THE OGILVIES.
THE HEAD OF THE FAMILY.

BY MRS. OLIPHANT.

THE CURATE IN CHARGE.
A SON OF THE SOIL.
YOUNG MUSGRAVE.
HE THAT WILL NOT WHEN HE MAY.
THE SECOND SON.
SIR TOM.
HESTER.
THE WIZARD'S SON.
A COUNTRY GENTLEMAN AND HIS FAMILY.

BY HUGH CONWAY.

A FAMILY AFFAIR. | LIVING OR DEAD.

BY HENRY JAMES.

PRINCESS CASAMASSIMA.
RODERICK HUDSON.
DAISY MILLER, etc. [etc.
THE MADONNA OF THE FUTURE,
WASHINGTON SQUARE.

BY THE AUTHOR OF "HOGAN, M.P."

HOGAN, M.P.
THE HON. MISS FERRARD.
CHRISTY CAREW.
ISMAY'S CHILDREN.
FLITTERS, TATTERS, AND THE COUNSELLOR: WEEDS, and other Sketches.

BY GEORGE FLEMING.

A NILE NOVEL.
MIRAGE.
VESTIGIA.
THE HEAD OF MEDUSA.

BY MRS. MACQUOID.

PATTY.

BY ANNIE KEARY.

JANET'S HOME.
OLDBURY.
A YORK AND A LANCASTER ROSE.
CLEMENCY FRANKLYN.

BY FRANCES H. BURNETT.

"LOUISIANA," AND "THAT LASS O' LOWRIE'S." Two Stories. | HAWORTH'S.

BY W. E. NORRIS.

CHRIS. | MY FRIEND JIM.

RAMONA: A Story. By HELEN JACKSON.
AUNT RACHEL. By D. CHRISTIE MURRAY.
A SLIP IN THE FENS.

Other Volumes to follow.

MACMILLAN AND CO., LONDON.

NEW NOVELS.

BY F. MARION CRAWFORD.

Sant' Ilario. By F. MARION CRAWFORD, Author of "With the Immortals," "Greifenstein," "Paul Patoff," "Mr. Isaacs," "Dr. Claudius," "Marzio's Crucifix," etc. 3 vols. Crown 8vo. 31s. 6d.

BY W. CLARK RUSSELL.

Marooned. By W. CLARK RUSSELL, Author of "The Wreck of the Grosvenor," etc. 3 vols. Crown 8vo. 31s. 6d.

MACMILLAN'S THREE SHILLING AND SIXPENNY NOVELS.
Crown 8vo.

Schwartz. By D. CHRISTIE MURRAY, Author of "Aunt Rachel," etc. Crown 8vo. 3s. 6d.

Neighbours on the Green. By Mrs. OLIPHANT. Crown 8vo. 3s. 6d.

Robbery under Arms; A Story of Life and Adventure in the Bush and in the Goldfields of Australia. By ROLF BOLDREWOOD. Crown 8vo. 3s. 6d.

The Weaker Vessel. By D. CHRISTIE MURRAY. Crown 8vo. 3s. 6d.

Joyce. By Mrs. OLIPHANT. Crown 8vo. 3s. 6d.

Cressy. By BRET HARTE. Crown 8vo. 3s. 6d.

Faithful and Unfaithful. By Margaret Lee, Author of "Dr. Wilmer's Love," "Lizzie Adriance," etc. Crown 8vo. 3s. 6d.

Reuben Sachs. By AMY LEVY, Author of "The Romance of a Shop." Crown 8vo. 3s. 6d.

Wessex Tales; Strange, Lively, and Commonplace. By THOMAS HARDY. Crown 8vo. 3s. 6d.

Miss Bretherton. By Mrs. HUMPHRY WARD, Author of "Robert Elsmere." Crown 8vo. 3s. 6d.

A London Life. By HENRY JAMES, Author of "The American," "The Europeans," "Daisy Miller," "The Reverberator," "The Aspern Papers." Crown 8vo. 3s. 6d.

Other Volumes to follow.

MACMILLAN AND CO., LONDON.

DATE DUE

www.ingramcontent.com/pod-product-compliance
Lightning Source LLC
Chambersburg PA
CBHW030255240426
43673CB00040B/979